ANTIDOTE

EXHILARATING
ENLIGHTENING
ELEVATING

ANTIDOTE
A JOURNEY HOMEWARD BOUND

ANURA PATEL

www.whitefalconpublishing.com

Antidote
Anura Patel

www.whitefalconpublishing.com

All rights reserved
First Edition, 2022
© Anura Patel, 2022
Cover design by White Falcon Publishing, 2022
Cover image source by Evgeni Tcherkasski on Unsplash.com

No part of this publication may be reproduced, or stored in a retrieval system, or transmitted in any form by means of electronic, mechanical, photocopying or otherwise, without prior written permission from the author.

The contents of this book have been certified and timestamped on the Gnosis blockchain as a permanent proof of existence. Scan the QR code or visit the URL given on the back cover to verify the blockchain certification for this book.

The views expressed in this work are solely those of the author and do not reflect the views of the publisher, and the publisher hereby disclaims any responsibility for them.

Requests for permission should be addressed to
anura.patel@gmail.com

ISBN - 978-1-63640-760-9

This book is devoted to
my spiritual gurus, guardians
and guiding lights;
Brahmaswarup Pramukh Swami Maharaj
and Pragat Brahmaswarup
Mahant Swami Maharaj.

Deeply indebted to the principles of
BAPS Swaminarayan Sanstha
for being the vision and
inspiration behind the book.

In loving memory of my uncle
Sidhu Patel

Contents

Preface xi

1. A Paradox Worth Pondering............................ 1
2. Five Senses of the Soul 7
3. Cooperation Transcends Competition 41
4. Home ward Bound 47
5. Vedas: The Gateway to Divinity 57
6. Upanishads: The Knowledge Divine............... 65
7. Sanskrit Language and its Contribution 101
8. Quantum Science & Ancient Indian Wisdom.. 131
9. A Spiritual Master Unprecedented 147
10. Mandirs: Connectors to the Cosmos 163
11. The Wonder that is Ayurveda 171

Epilogue.. 189

Preface

The genesis of this book draws inspiration from observing the everyday life as much as imbibing from the evolved minds. In the recent past, I listened to Mr. Sai Deepak, a bright young mind, on the topic of recontextualizing history. What he spoke is an eye opener for all Indians especially the youth in whose hands lie the future destiny of this great nation. He said that majority of the people should have a shared view of the past, at least an overlap of aspirations for the future to be called a nation. Further elaborating on the subject, he said that, History plays a major role in establishing identity. Without history one has no roots or identity. People present now, cannot be held responsible for what their forefathers did. In India, the problem is that truth and reconciliation have never been a part of the discourse nor has it been published in history books in the truest sense of the word. Our history books only mention the invasions that we have faced in the last 1200 years and so a child grows up feeling that he is a product of a defeated nation. His or her self-esteem is damaged.

A lot of young people are awakening to this change. In the beginning, people from the humanities started talking about it and soon were joined by scientists, engineers, doctors, and others who with a natural lean towards logic and reason were able to throw light on the subject leveraging their strong base in research, facts and figures. Many young intellectuals in India and abroad have joined this Indic renaissance movement. One of the most influential persons who has single handedly contributed a lot in this area is Mr. Rajeev Malhotra. He is still moving ahead in a powerful way. His talks and books have created required changes and aroused interest in many young people who in turn are also working for this very noble cause. For me, listening to him and reading his book "Battle for Sanskrit" has created a sense of pride for my country, its culture, and traditions. It also motivated me to learn this beautiful language.

In this book, I have tried to cover topics which purely belong to this soil and are the foundations of our civilization and culture. India is one of the oldest civilizations in the world and has significantly contributed to the world. Many foreign historians, authors and philosophers who have had a chance to know our culture, traditions, customs through translations or originals have experienced transformation like never before. Such is the power and influence of this great culture. Having a dip in it acts like an antidote, protecting us from detrimental effects of extreme materialism. It provides us with a sense of balance and stability in this dynamic environment, we are facing every moment.

Our goal in this human journey becomes crystal clear, for we are truth seekers. Our purpose in life is expansion of consciousness and not just gaining material pleasure. Keeping this in mind, this book is a succinct articulation of the many subjects which personally have had a very positive impact on my mind, heart and way of life. Wish it does the same to all those who read this book.

No work is possible without cooperation. Isolation breeds mediocrity. This book would not have materialized without the support of my many well-wishers. I am especially grateful to my sister, Avani, for her immense support throughout the project. Her insightful inputs have really helped me to further the purpose of this book writing journey of mine. Without her design acumen, the cover page and chapter pages of my book wouldn't have looked so beautiful! I am equally thankful to my family for their support and encouragement. Gratitude.

Sincerely hope for the readers to enjoy their journey through the book.

CHAPTER 1

A PARADOX WORTH PONDERING

Antidote

> ***"The two most Important days in your life are the day you are born and the day you find out why"***
>
> *– Mark Twain*

I have read the following lines many a times and it has had an overpowering effect on my mind. The author is not George Carlin as usually mentioned but Dr. Bob Moorhead, former Pastor of Seattle's Over lake Christian church. He retired in 1998 after 29 years in post. He wrote this as a backdrop to spreading aftermath of 1999 columbine shooting.

"The paradox of our time in history is that we have taller buildings but shorter tempers, wider freeways but narrower viewpoints. We spend more but have less. We buy more but enjoy less. We have bigger houses and smaller families. We have more degrees and less sense. More knowledge but less judgement. More medicine and less wellness. We have multiplied our possessions but reduced our values. We love too seldom and hate too often. We have learnt to make a living but not a life. We have added years to life but not life to years. We have been all the way to the moon but have trouble crossing the street to meet a new neighbor. We conquered outer space but not inner space. We have done larger things but not better things. We have cleaned up the air but polluted our souls. We have conquered the atom but we are prejudiced. These are times of fast food and slow digestion. Big men and small character. Steep profits and shallow relationships. These are the days of two incomes but more divorces. Fancier houses but broken homes. These are the days of quick trips and disposable diapers. Throw away morality and one-night stands. Times where there is much in the showroom and nothing in the stock room[1].

I request you to stop reading and sincerely ponder on above lines. So, what do you think? Are we disconnected from reality that we have ceased being human? We have fallen into a deep chasm, so when we look around all we see is outer glamour, rat race and superficiality. We see this everywhere and believe it to be okay. This is how life should be. It is the same all around us. We have moved away from nature and towards everything artificial. This is not a case against materialism but balance is always sought between extremes. According to the Persian poet Rumi, "Anything which is more than our necessity is poison. It may be power, wealth, hunger, ego, greed, laziness, love, ambition, hate

---

1 https://www.psychologytoday.com/us/blog/the-resilient-brain/201901/the-paradox-our-time-or-timeless-paradox

or anything."[2] We are in need of deep introspection. Most of our lives are spent on a material plane. Our thoughts are related to our finite body and our perishable possessions. Very few ponder over things above the mundane. We need to look inward. Compared to outward progress our inward progress is very less. When we behold the vast universe with our limited senses, whatever little we observe leaves us spellbound. Using instruments of science, humans have tried to delve into mysteries of the cosmos and have ended up having little success. It is like observing the tip of an iceberg. Astronauts orbiting around our blue planet are mesmerized by its beauty and get overwhelmed by the emotions they experience. The ugly part taking place on the earth is obscured from view. Everything on earth looks so beautiful, so peaceful and so tranquil. Then why the dark side? Why the greed and selfishness? This planet is our home and as its custodians it is the joint duty of all inhabitants to protect and nurture it. Then why do we not reach clear solutions?

Rabindranath Tagore has beautifully explained it. He says, "when children begin to learn each separate letter of the alphabet, they find no real pleasure in it, because they miss the real purpose of the lesson.

---

2   http://beyondtheopposites.com/2017/10/23/rumi-on-poison/#sthash.WTyUqeZ7.k5GVvUUT.dpbs

While letters claim our attention only in themselves as isolated things, they fatigue us. They become the source of joy to us when they combine into words and sentences to convey an idea. Likewise, our soul when detached and imprisoned within narrow limits of self loses its significance for its very essence is unity.[3] One can find out the truth by unifying with others. The real purpose of life is to become one with the Cosmos. Our universe is alive and conscious. It is with this consciousness we all exist on earth. Our main problem is, we only believe in what all of us perceive with senses. These senses have their own limitations. Throwing light on this Mahatma Gandhi explains it very clearly, he says "Sense perception can be and often are false and deceptive, however real they may appear to us. Where there is realization outside the senses, it is infallible. It is proved not by extraneous evidence but in the transformed conduct and character of those who have felt the real presence of God within."[4]

---

3   The Great Works of Rabindranath Tagore – Page 412
4   https://www.brainyquote.com/quotes/mahatma_gandhi_700530

CHAPTER 2

FIVE SENSES OF THE SOUL

Photo by Daiga Ellaby on Unsplash

Antidote

"The wise man beholds all beings in the self and the self in all beings for that reason he does not hate anyone."[5]

– Isha Upanishad

श्रद्धावांल्लभते ज्ञानं तत्परंः संयतेन्द्रियः ।
ज्ञानं लब्ध्वा परां शान्ति-मचिरेणाधिगच्छति ꠰ 4/39 Bhagvad Geeta

Those who's faith is deep and who have practiced controlling their mind and senses attain divine knowledge.

Through such transcendental knowledge they quickly attain everlasting supreme peace.

The spirit cannot be bound by these five senses for it is inherently free. It is futile to try and use these sense perceptions to seek the spirit and beyond. Our souls can be reached by intuition, peace, foresight, faith, and empathy. This five-sense perception of soul exists but is obscured from our view and experience due to a thin veil of ignorance. This veil has been uncovered for many who persevered and have undergone sadhana to view the beauty of the soul.

---

5 https://upanishads.home.blog/2019/04/14/the-self-in-all-beings-isa-upanishad-verse-6/

The above five virtues when practiced help in expansion of consciousness by putting aside and forgetting petty issues which consume a lot of our precious time. We are raised to uncharted heights on the path of enlightenment or self-realization. We have heard about intuition many times but are imprisoned by limitations and believe intuition to bless only a few. Each of us has intuition. What is intuition? It is the combination of insight and imagination attributed to spiritual communication. In intuition the mind becomes aware without direct intervention of reason. Intuition is the truest energy for what your spirit is feeling. It bridges the gap between subconscious and conscious mind. If we pay attention and remain calm, we can perceive it. Today's digital devices and mainly cell phones have stifled intuition. Stress and competition also smother intuition. Intuition can be effectively approached by practicing mindfulness, that is to focus on being in the moment or call it presence of mind. The second thing is to trust your gut feeling. Many times, in our experience we have made decisions based on gut feeling. Logic or reason would have had no place and still was proved right. Albert Einstein explains what intuition is in a very appropriate way by saying, "the intuitive mind is a sacred gift and a rational mind is a faithful servant.

We have created a society that honors the servant and has forgotten the gifts."[6]

Intuition is a faculty of higher intelligence or spiritual mind. It is a kind of higher mental awareness. The purer the mind greater the ability to process the information and provide insight into the nature of things. Being intuitive is proof that the soul is connected to a higher power. Intuition transcends reason. It acquires knowledge directly and in a holistic way whereas Intellect mainly follows reductionism. According to Dr. Radhakrishnan[7] intuition is an integral experience. It is integral in the sense that it coordinates and synthesizes all other experiences into a more unified whole. Intuition goes beyond logic to reveal previous unseen connection between facts. The presupposition of spiritualism is that the human mind has the capacity to relate to a non-material realm where limitations of time and space do not apply hence intuitive knowledge is holistic. One example of a highly intuitive mind is that of Shri Nivas Ramanujan the mathematical genius who made substantial contributions to analytical theory of numbers elliptical functions, continued fraction and infinite series and

---

6 https://www.goodreads.com/author/quotes/36825.Gary_Klein
7 http://dspace.jgu.edu.in:8080/jspui/bitstream/10739/2887/1/S%20Radhakrishnan%20Integral%20Experience.pdf

proved more than 3000 mathematical theorems in his short life span.

Professor Hardy, a renowned Mathematician at Cambridge university to whom Ramanujan wrote a letter, including his theorems was in complete awe. He said, "Ramanujan combined a power of generalization, a feeling for form and a capacity for rapid modification of his hypothesis that were often really startling and made him in his peculiar field without a rival in his days. The limitations of his knowledge were startling as his profundity. Here was a man who could work out modular equations and theorems to orders unheard of, who's mastery of continued fraction was beyond that of any mathematician in the world, who had found for himself the functional equation of the zeta function and the dominant terms of many of the most famous problems in the analytic theory of numbers, yet he had never heard of a doubly periodic function or of Cauchy's theorem and indeed had the vaguest idea of what a function of a complex variable was". Ramanujan did not have the basic tools which mathematicians had; he did not build his work on the work of others but rather seemed to just invent for himself. He compiled some 3900 mathematical results during his lifetime. After his death nearly all his claims have been proven true, opening entirely new areas of study, and inspiring much further study research. He was the first Indian to be elected fellow of Trinity college Cambridge. Years after his death Hardy was asked to rate prominent mathematicians based on pure talent using scale one to hundred. Hardy gave himself a 25. His colleague and friend J.E Littlewood a 30. The legendary German Mathematician David Hilbert an 80. To Shri Nivas Ramanujan he gave a 100. His influence was so prominent that a scientific journal was published in his name "The Ramanujan Journal." As math and science have developed and evolved, Ramanujan's work has become relevant to avenues to study which did not even exist when he was alive. These areas were computer science, electrical engineering, and study of black holes. During his time nobody knew black holes were something to study, yet Ramanujan had already developed a formula which would be used to describe their properties generations later. As mathematician Ken Ono of Emory University (Atlanta Georgia) recently described "Ramanujan's formula has offered glimpses into theories that Ramanujan probably would not have been able to articulate himself, theories nobody needed until they needed them. How would Ramanujan know about the things that did not exist? How was he able to provide insight so far beyond what was understood in his time"? Ono said, "it is inconceivable he had this intuition but he must have". Fellow mathematician Freeman Dyson of Institute of Advanced Study at Princeton said, "He had some sort of magic trick we do not understand.

Perhaps there was a factor we do not understand at work. Not magic but something else." Ramanujan always said "an equation has for me no meaning unless it represents a thought of God.

Ramanujan stated that the insight of his work came to him in his dreams on many occasions. Throughout his life he repeatedly dreamed of a Hindu Goddess Namakkal (Maha Laxmi). She presented him with complex mathematical formulas over and over which he would then test and verify upon waking. One such example was the infinite series, Pi. Describing one of his many math dreams Ramanujan said, "While asleep I had an unusual experience, there was a red screen with blood flowing. I was observing it. Suddenly a hand began writing on it. I became all attention. The hand wrote several results in elliptical integrals. They stuck in my mind. As soon as I woke up, I committed them to writing.

The creator of periodic table Russian chemist Dmitri Mendeleev said that it came to him in a dream that all the elements including some that were not discovered simply fell in place before him. Albert Einstein was famous for his thought experiment where he would sit in quiet solitude and imagine the results of theoretical concepts. It was during one of these thought experiments, he came up with the famous equation $E=MC^2$. There is one explanation, one which goes beyond magic or serendipity. The explanations are somethings called Akashic Records, from Sanskrit word Akasha meaning essence of all things in material world. Plato and Aristotle called it quint essence. Akashic Records are universal data bases of all human knowledge and experience. This database is said to be in a higher plane of existence and is available to be accessed by anyone at any time. Perhaps the most fervent supporter of the existence of Akashic Records is none other than Nicola Tesla. In his book "Man's Greatest Achievements" published in 1907 he writes, "All perceptible matter comes from a primary substance or tenuity beyond conception, filling all space, the Akasha or Luminiferous ether which is acted upon by the life-giving prana or creative force, calling it into existence in a never-ending cycle of all things and phenomena. Tesla said, "My brain is only a receiver in the universe, there is a core from which we obtain knowledge, strength, and inspiration. I have not penetrated secrets of this core, but I know it exists".[8]

Intuition works only when one is pure in heart and mind. Baser passions in humans veil intuition so that it remains hidden and dormant. I feel we are intuitive when our soul connects with the cosmic energy which is the source of all knowledge. In fact,

---

8   Excerpt from https://www.youtube.com/watch?v=xGfV80ioA6U

intuition is the way primitive tribes survive in hostile conditions. There are skills used for survival based on intuition in the natural world. The tribal people live disconnected from our modern world. They have comparatively purer minds for intuition to work as their necessities are less and are more content in life. There is oral transfer of knowledge regarding medicinal plants, hunting skills, reading nature signs, navigation through the forest and more. There is a holistic approach to the above knowledge system necessary for them to survive in remote areas. Tribal people very well understand that in order to face challenges and adversity they will have to have to work in cooperation. For the welfare of the whole tribe selfish motives are replaced by higher benevolent causes. They remain connected with one another and with nature blending in the larger cosmic plan to avoid disturbances. This is the reason they live peacefully and contently. I feel animals, birds and isolated tribal people live within the rules laid down by nature. They do not challenge nature but live in sync with it. They contribute towards conservation of our environment.

Such places contribute to peaceful coexistence. Peace emanates all around. There is an insightful shloka from Maha Upanishad which says,

Antidote

अयं निजः परो वेति गणना लघु चेतसाम् ।
उदारचरितानां तु वसुधैव कुटुम्बकम् ।

This is mine and this is yours say, the small minded.
The wise believe the whole world to be a family.

All fights, acts of violence and wars have resulted from I and Mine. We have isolated ourselves and created walls whereas what we need is bridges. To connect with one and all and to understand each other is necessary for peace. Peace must spring from within then only can its effects be experienced from outside. Calm and peace-loving thoughts are precursors of peace actualized on the outside.

I came upon a beautiful parable which illustrated in depth the real meaning of peace. There was a king in olden ages who had a fascination for paintings. He offered a handsome prize to any painter whose painting would depict 'peace'. Many painters brought their art to the king on the day of judgement. The king had a thorough look at all the paintings and then he ordered two paintings to be placed aside. One painting had a lake with calm waters, clear sky and a few fluffy clouds and mountains. The second was just the opposite. There was a dark overcast sky, thundering waterfalls, rushing rivers, streaks of lightning and a dark mountain. The king looked closely at the side of the mountain and saw on the branch of a tree overlooking a valley, a small nest and there was a mother bird feeding its young ones affectionately. The king chose the second picture. Peace is not absence of noise or violence. Peace is to be in a calm state in midst of chaos and mayhem, to stay focused and maintain our inner stability.

Eckhart Tolle, a spiritual teacher, and author has said "you find peace not by rearranging the circumstances of your life but realizing who you are at the deepest level."[9] We are proud inheritors of a culture and civilization which for ages has promoted the ideals for peace. Our sacred scriptures, Vedas and Upanishads begin with peace chants or prayers. One of many peace chants that has touched my being is from Yajur Veda (36:17)

ॐ द्यौः शान्तिरन्तरिक्षं शान्तिः
पृथिवी शान्तिरापः शान्तिरोषधयः शान्तिः ।
वनस्पतयः शान्तिर्विश्वेदेवाः शान्तिर्ब्रह्म शान्तिः
सर्व शान्तिः शान्तिरेव शान्तिः सा मा शान्तिरेधि ।।
ॐ शान्तिः शान्तिः शान्तिः ।।

*May there me peace in sky and peace in space
between earth and sky, peace on earth and water,
in plants and trees, in deities presiding over nature*

---

9 https://healingbrave.com/blogs/all/eckhart-tolle-quotes-peace

Antidote

*let peace pervade everywhere inside and out,
may you be established in peace.*

Another very popular shanti mantra is from
Taitteriya Upanishad

ॐ सह नाववतु । सह नौ भुनक्तु ।
सह वीर्यं करवावहै ।
तेजस्वि नावधीतमस्तु मा विद्विषावहै ।
ॐ शान्तिः शान्तिः शान्तिः ॥

May god protect us both together, may God nourish us both together, may we work conjointly with great energy, may our study be vigorous and effective, may we not mutually hate let there be peace in me, let there be peace in my environment, let there be peace in forces acting on me. The above peace mantra was chanted at the ashrama where students spent a long time in studies. It was of utmost importance to establish peace between the master and the pupil to ensure a smooth flow of communication from teacher to student and the other way also. Isolation and selfishness were never a part of Vedic culture. The Rishis always practiced harmony and taught the same to their pupils.

Peace is possible only if we practice the ideal of 'Ahimsa' that is nonviolence. In Ahimsa one overrides the impulse to hate and hold love for one and all. Our scriptures describe Ahimsa as one of the highest moral virtues. A person who practices Ahimsa in its purest form has the whole world at his or her feet. Our scriptures brim with incidents where venomous snakes and wild ferocious animals have forsaken their inherent violent nature and have become docile when they encountered sages. The ancient hermitages are befitting examples. Bhagwan Swaminarayan as young Neelkanth Yogi on his way to great Himalayas was meditating outside an Ashram in a place called Sripur. The head ascetic of the ashram requested Neelkanth Yogi to come inside the ashram for the night as there was fear of a lion roaming nearby. Neelkanth Yogi was fearless, clearly Ahimsa was a way of life for him. He refused to go inside and sat meditating under a huge tree. The lion did come at night but to the astonishment of the head Sanyasi he sat down in front of young Neelkanth Yogi and as dawn arrived, he vanished into the nearby forest. Ahimsa is a universal ideal. It transcends place, time, and race. Those who practice ahimsa exuberate peace. It is the highest self-control.

The Shandilya Upanishad lists ten forbearances in which Ahimsa is the first and then come Satya, Asteya, Brahmacharya, Daya, Arjava, Kshama, Druti, Mitahara and Saucha, meaning Truth, No stealing, Celibacy, Compassion, Sincerity, Forgiveness, Fortitude, Balanced diet, Purity of mind body and speech.

Antidote

अहिंसा परमो धर्मस तथाहिंसा परो दमः ।
अहिंसा परमं दानम अहिंसा परमस तपः ।
अहिंसा परमो यज्ञस तथाहिस्मा परं बलम ।
अहिंसा परमं मित्रम अहिंसा परमं सुखम ।
अहिंसा परमं सत्यम अहिंसा परमं शरुतम ।।

The above verse from Mahabharat (Mahaprasthanika Parva) describes Ahimsa as the highest virtue, highest self-control, greatest gift, best austerity, highest sacrifice, highest strength, greatest friend, greatest happiness, highest truth, and greatest teaching.

We can talk of nonviolence and peace. We have conferences and high-end meetings and summits on world peace. Since its inception in 1945 (24th October) UNO is trying hard to lessen violence and terrorism in the world and establish peace. How far has it succeeded? In fact, terrorism, wars and civil wars still ravage the world and show no sign of regression. Wars start in the minds of men. The average human mind has narrowed its limits to I and Mine. Borders in our psych create borders on land. The question is, do we really want peace? If we do, then the need arises to clean up our inner environment, only then can we see the results we so dearly want to see on the exterior.

I would like to share with you all an inspiring incident of how one person's positive and peaceful demeanor and proper response to an adversity of large scale avoided a man made calamity of heights unknown. The incident goes back to year 2002 in the month of September. Gandhinagar the capital of Gujarat was busy with the usual hustle and bustle. Situated in Gandhinagar is Akshardham Monument, a beautiful landmark adorning the capital. It represents thousands of years of Indian culture and heritage. The main shrine is where the magnificent Pancha Dhatu murti of Bhagwan Swaminarayan is blessing all who come in faith and devotion. It was built under the inspiration of Pramukh Swami Maharaj of BAPS Sanstha. Akshardham is a symbol of peace and unity. It is the voice of many visitors to have experienced utter peace and joy upon entering the sacred premises. The complex was busy as usual with visitors all over the place. On 24th September two terrorists planned to attack this sacred site. They managed to enter the complex and fire mercilessly killing thirty-one visitors including a sadhu of BAPS Sanstha. Seventy visitors were wounded, some of them seriously. The NSG commandos arrived at 11pm and started operation thunderbolt, which lasted till 6:45 am next morning. Both the terrorists were killed and one NSG commando was critically injured. He remained in coma for 2 years before passing away. The nation was in shock and so was Gujarat. There was anger mixed with great sadness and Pramukh Swami Maharaj was surrounded by people voicing different responses to this shameful act. Some voiced strong protests against this attack and sought retaliation. The atmosphere was charged with hatred and thoughts of revenge. However, Swamiji remained calm and composed and chose the path of prayer and forgiveness. This did not mean inactivity. He did all he had to do. He comforted the injured in the hospital and prayed for those who were unfortunate and had lost their lives. He visited the monument and surveyed the damage. He instructed the persons in charge for its quick repair and clean up. To everyone's astonishment Akshardham was reopened to public on 7th of October. On the night of the attack Swamiji's message was broadcasted Nationally and Internationally, wherein he appealed to the people to maintain peace. He did not utter a single word which was out of place as it would have signaled out reasons for communal riots across Gujarat and India. He did not let this happen. This is Ahimsa in real form and action. Swamiji's words were powerful yet so serene that people chose to maintain peace and order in midst of chaos. Gujarat was saved from a major man-made calamity. Swamiji's foresight also played a very important role in this situation.

Foresightedness is a crucial quality which decides a secured and bright future. Following are a few quotes by great personalities. These are elevating, inspiring and soul stirring ideas expressed by great people to lift our spirit and encourage us to move ahead in right direction.

> "As a single foot step will not make a path in earth so a single thought will not make a pathway in the mind. To make a deep physical path we walk again and again. To make a deep mental path we must think over and over the kind of thoughts we wish we to dominate our lives."[10]
>
> *Henry David Thoreau*

> "Once you make a decision the universe conspires to make it happen."[11]
>
> *Ralph Waldo Emerson*

> "The object of education is to give men the unity of truth, I believe in a spiritual world not anything seperate but as its inner most truth. With the breath we draw we must always feel this trust that we are living in God."[12]
>
> *Rabindranath Tagore*

---

10 https://www.azquotes.com/author/14637-Henry_David_Thoreau
11 https://www.azquotes.com/quote/89257
12 https://www.learnreligions.com/tagore-quotes-about-god-1770326

"The highest education is that which does not merely give us information but makes our life in harmony with existence."[13]

Rabindranath Tagore

"Everything comes to us that belongs to us, if we create the capacity to receive it."[14]

Rabindranath Tagore

"Take up one idea, make that one idea your life, think of it, dream of it, live on that idea, let the brain muscles, nerves every part of your body be full of that idea and just leave every other idea alone. This is the way to succeed and this is the way great spiritual giants are produced."[15]

Swami Vivekananda

"That man has reached immortality who is disturbed by nothing material."[16]

Swami Vivekananda

---

13 https://www.brainyquote.com/quotes/rabindranath_tagore_389999
14 https://www.brainyquote.com/quotes/rabindranath_tagore_385179
15 https://www.brainyquote.com/quotes/swami_vivekananda_213397
16 https://www.brainyquote.com/quotes/swami_vivekananda_213407

"Each work must pass three stages ridicule, opposition and then acceptance. Those who think ahead of their times are sure to be misunderstood."[17]

Swami Vivekananda

"Whatever you believe that you will be. If you believe yourself to be sages, sages you will be tomorrow. There is nothing to obstruct you."[18]

Swami Vivekananda

"If I love my self despite my infinite faults, how can I hate anyone at a glimpse of a few faults."[19]

Swami Vivekananda

"Our human compassion binds us one to the other not in pity or patronizingly but as human beings who have learnt how to turn our common suffering into hope for future."[20]

Nelson Mandela

---

17 https://www.goodreads.com/quotes/281266
18 https://quotefancy.com/quote/913563/Swami-Vivekananda
19 https://twitter.com/insprepositive/status/1297364336558579712/photo/1
20 https://www.brainyquote.com/quotes/nelson_mandela_447262

"If future generations are to remember us with more gratitude than sorrow, we must achieve more than just the miracles of technology. We must also leave them a glimpse of the world as it was created, not just as it looked when we got through with it."[21]

Lyndon B. Johnson

"If a country is to be corruption free and become a nation of beautiful minds, I strongly feel there are three key societal members who can make a difference they are the father, the mother and the teacher."[22]

APJ Abdul Kalam

"While children are struggling to be unique the world around them is trying by all means to make them look like everybody else."[23]

APJ Abdul Kalam

---

21 https://www.brainyquote.com/quotes/lyndon_b_johnson_144728
22 https://www.brainyquote.com/quotes/a_p_j_abdul_kalam_178502
23 https://www.brainyquote.com/quotes/a_p_j_abdul_kalam_589719

"All wars signify the failure of conflict resolution mechanisms and they need post war rebuilding of faith, trust and confidence."[24]

APJ Abdul Kalam

"Man falls from the pursuit of the ideal of plain living and high thinking the moment he wants to multiply his daily wants. Man's happiness really lies in contentment."[25]

Mahatma Gandhi

"God cannot be realized through intellect. Intellect can lead one to a certain extent and no further. It is a matter of faith and experience derived from that faith."[26]

Mahatma Gandhi

"Our greatest ability as humans is not to change the world but to change our selves."[27]

Mahatma Gandhi

---

24 https://www.brainyquote.com/quotes/a_p_j_abdul_kalam_589743
25 https://www.brainyquote.com/quotes/mahatma_gandhi_160874
26 https://www.brainyquote.com/quotes/mahatma_gandhi_629306
27 https://www.azquotes.com/quote/850719

"The difference between what we do and what we are capable of doing would suffice to solve most of the world's problems."[28]

Mahatma Gandhi

"Morality is the basis of things and truth is the substance of all morality."[29]

Mahatma Gandhi

"I believe that Gandhi's views were most enlightened of all political men of our time. We should strive to do things in his spirit. Not to use violence in fighting for our cause but by non-participation in anything you believe is evil."[30]

Albert Einstein

"Inspiration is a slender river of brightness leaping from a vast and eternal knowledge, it exceeds reason more perfectly than reason exceeds the knowledge of the senses."[31]

Sri Aurobindo

---

[28] https://www.brainyquote.com/quotes/mahatma_gandhi_150718
[29] https://www.brainyquote.com/quotes/mahatma_gandhi_160769
[30] https://www.goodreads.com/quotes/321355
[31] https://www.quotemaster.org/qc7e16127ac794c6f6c8364a3df305706

"Spiritual unfoldment cannot take place merely because of an intellectual appreciation of theory of perfection. Evolution takes place only when a corresponding change in the subjective life is accomplished."[32]

Swami Chinmayananda

"To listen is not merely to hear. We, in life, hear but very rarely do we know how to listen. To listen is to hear with an intellectual alertness and attention of awareness."[33]

Swami Chinmayananda

"In the joy of others lies our own,
In the progress of others rests our own,
In the good of others abides our own,
Know this to be the key to peace and happiness."[34]

Pramukh Swami Maharaj

"God is not our reflection but we are His reflection. Because of him we are great and glorious, our powers have been given by Him, everything is His."[35]

Pramukh Swami Maharaj

---

32 https://quotepark.com/quotes/1722383
33 https://libquotes.com/chinmayananda-saraswati/quote/lby4j1l
34 https://www.goodreads.com/quotes/7401385
35 http://www.swaminarayan.org/vicharan/2001/07/02/index.htm

All the above ideas carry a lot of substance. If imbibed and put in practical use can lead us out of adversities and shape for us a secured future. They come from an experiential plane together with knowledge. It is not possible for all of us to reach heights great men did, but acquiring a little from such a colossal treasury can make a difference in the way we look at life. We may not be able to see results immediately but with faith and perseverance we will be able to see the change we want.

Faith is loosely translated as 'Shraddha' in Sanskrit. Shraddha has a much deeper meaning to it. It is that innate emotion, a very profound one. It is powerful and yet so delicate. The whole universe including our beautiful planet Earth inspires us to have faith. Looking at the precise working of the universe, a strong sense of trust arises in our hearts, trust in the creator, for there cannot be such order such splendor and magnificence without Him. Emerson has rightly said "All I have seen teaches me to trust the creator for all that I have not seen."[36] Dr. Abdul Kalam, though a scientist, was a man of faith. Once he quoted, "When God pushes you to the edge of difficulty trust him fully because two things can happen either he

---

36 https://www.brainyquote.com/quotes/ralph_waldo_emerson_118592

will catch you when you fall or he will teach you how to fly."[37] We always believe what we see or hear because we rely on our sensory perception. But the idea "believe to see" is totally the other way around, it transcends the physical realm.

The physical eyes will not be able to visualize what the seers or sages saw with their inner eyes or eyes of the soul. Faith in the initial stage is simple belief. To keep the faith firm and moving we need a Guru with these divine qualities. Spiritual Sadhana is no easy path. The enlightened Guru knows the way and so it would be easy for a spiritual aspirant to follow the Master's footsteps. Deep study of our scriptures (Adhyayan) further instills and nurtures our faith.

Charles Steinmetz an electrical engineer and pioneer of air condition system said "I think the greatest discoveries will be made along spiritual lines. Someday day people will realize that material things do not bring happiness. The scientists of the world will turn their labs over to the study of God and prayer. When that day comes the world will see more advancement in one generation than it has seen in the last four."[38]

---

[37] https://www.searchquotes.com/quotation/When_God_pushes_you_to_the_edge_of_difficulty

[38] https://www.baps.org/Article/2011/Spirituality-The-Greatest-Force-Of-Mankind-Part-1--2035.aspx

Antidote

The above lines are capable of instilling tremendous faith if we have strong conviction and we try to incorporate these ideals in our lives. Faith has no relation with proof or reason. What we see in the holy Geeta is that Shri Krishna works on Arjuna's mind by slowly instilling deep faith in him. In the beginning Arjuna is dejected and filled with sorrow and remorse. He cannot think clearly and is overwhelmed by emotions so much so that he starts perspiring and his famous Gandiva bow slips down from his hand. The mighty warrior sits down and declares "न योत्स्य" I will not fight. From here Bhagwan Shri Krishna empowers Arjuna in different ways through 700 verses we journey in the Shrimad Bhagwat Geeta. There is a complete transformation in Arjuna, where he at last declares "करिष्ये वचनं तव" I will do as you say. Shri Krishna says,

" सर्वधर्मान्यरित्यज्य मामेकं शरणं व्रज ।
अहं त्वा सर्वपापेभ्यो मोक्षयिष्यामि मा शुच ": ॥ 18.66

Put aside all your beliefs and surrender to me, I will release you from all your sins and liberate you so have no fear. Throughout the Geeta we find the element of faith ripening in Arjuna's heart. Faith in the divine helps us overcome obstacles in life. Faith is an invisible support system which also instills a strong sense of courage when things in life are far from smooth. Faith inspires one to have patience or fortitude and helps to keep negative emotions in check. Faith along with tolerance can help us override many mishaps in life. Some of the burning issues in our society like suicide, divorces, and domestic violence are the result of absence of the above virtues. In olden days the foundation of society lay in spiritual ideals. The method was holistic and ensured smooth functioning of day-to-day affairs. Today's scenario is quite different looking at the fast pace globalization clutching all. We are under the cringe of cultural identity. To be honest we are ashamed of our traditions, customs, rituals, and way of worship. The influence of western ideas has overshadowed our original thinking and way of life. We have become master imitators not realizing the damaging effect it has on our psyche. Imitators are never respected. We can be global citizens and yet remain loyal to our culture and heritage. We must reawaken our faith in our ancient wisdom.

If we take stock of our gains and losses, a very grim picture faces us. We may have advanced technologically to stay amid gadgets and get everything done at the press of a button. Artificial intelligence is the big talk in recent times and robots have started replacing humans. We all take pride at this progress, forgetting the dangers that accompany. Children are losing sensitivity and uncensored media violence and easily available pornography sites on electronic gadgets have created havoc in homes. Self-centeredness and self- gratification have diminished our sensitivity and creativity. Where does all this point to? I feel one of the reasons is a lack of empathy. Once you lose empathy you lose humanity. Stephen Covey says, "When you show deep empathy towards others their defensive energy goes down and positive energy replaces it. That is when you can get more creative in solving the problems."[39]

Empathy is the highest form of intelligence; it is a faculty which resonates with other feelings. Dr Kalam said "I am not a handsome guy but I can give my hand to someone who needs help."[40] He demonstrated empathy which was natural to him. Empathy used to be an ability inherent in Indian culture but it is sad to see this ebbing away at an alarming rate. During the times of calamity or crisis we do observe people helping the needy in different ways. There is an intrinsic site in the human heart wherein dwells empathy. David Hume said "The minds of men are mirrors to one another"[41] Empathy is not exactly compassion but compassion cannot

---

39 https://www.brainyquote.com/quotes/stephen_covey_636538
40 https://www.goodreads.com/quotes/787493-i-am-not-handsome-but-i-can-give-my-hand
41 https://www.azquotes.com/quote/692790

take place without empathy as it requires a high degree of emotional awareness and emotional sensitivity.

Although there may be individual differences in empathy based on genetic differences, research suggests it is possible to boost the capacity for empathic understanding. In recent years neuroscientists have advanced the concept of mirror neurons which are believed to enhance capacity to display, read and mimic emotional signals through facial expressions and other forms of body language, mirror neurons may help individuals to share experiences and become more empathetic towards others.[42]

I read a short story which really touched my heart. A farmer was putting up a sign which stated he had four pups for sale. He was nailing the sign and felt a tug on his side and turned around to see a young boy. The boy requested the farmer to give him one pup. The farmer said it would cost money as the pup boasted of a good pedigree. The boy reached into his pocket and took out some change which amounted to 39 cents and gave it to the farmer. The farmer called out to the mother dog and out she came followed by four balls of fur. After a while another pup followed

---

[42] Excerpt from psychologytoday.com-speaking tree

hobbling awkwardly. The boy requested the farmer to give him that pup. The farmer gently told the boy that he would not want a pup which would not be able to run and play with him. The young boy pulled up his trousers and revealed the steel braces on both legs and specially made shoes. He looked up again at the farmer and said, "You see sir, I don't run too well myself and he will need someone who understands." I strongly feel that empathy is outright natural in kids but as they grow the environment affects it. If circumstances arise under the practical demands of modern life, it is compromised and gets stifled.

Dr. Abdul Kalam was one such man full of empathy. Once his bedroom in stately Rashtrapati Bhavan was found to be leaking. P.M. Nair, then secretary to the former president discovered to his shock when the latter called him up in the morning of July 14th, 2003 to say that he could not sleep because his bedroom ceiling was leaking. "Any other president and my head would have rolled though for no fault of mine" says Nair in a shuddering recall of annexure to his political memoir - The Kalam Effect" My years with the president, but thanks to Dr. Kalam's innate empathy he put his secretary to ease quickly. He said, "Do not worry, I know you will set things right in my bedroom but I am worried about those houses in the president's estate where they may not have a second bedroom to shift and the only one, they have leaks.[43]"

The second incident was narrated by Srijan Pal Singh who spent a lot of time with Dr. Kalam. He wrote about an incident back in 2004. Dr Kalam and Srijan Pal were visiting the Scottish city of Edinburg known worldwide for its research. They visited several laboratories and one of those was Anne Rowling Regenerative Neurology clinic headed by Professor Siddharthan Chandran. He showed them all the work being conducted in his small lab. The last researcher was working on fixing this problem called voice banking which would be used to store a person's voice and later be used to communicate with others. Dr. Kalam had particular interest in the said technology. He asked a series of questions to understand more and left saying he would like to know more about that technology. Srijan Pal was curious and asked Dr. Kalam why he was keen to know more on voice banking? He replied, "I have a friend, a wonderful man whom I respect a lot. He was a great orator once but now has great difficulty speaking clearly. I want to hear him speak beautifully

---

43 https://www.deccanchronicle.com/150730/nation-current-affairs/article/leaking-roof-and-kalam%E2%80%99s-empathy

again. You know who he is? Before I could answer he said Vajpayeeji.[44]"

Brene Brown says "Empathy has no script. There is no right or wrong way to do it is simply listening, holding space, withholding judgement, emotionally connecting, and communicating that incredible message of "you are not alone". The above lines mean a lot to me personally. The deeper essence has been etched permanently within my heart for I have experienced it intensely. My story goes back to the millennium year 2000. The world had just entered the 21st century. Human kind was celebrating a historic moment in time. For me the last few months were a bit too difficult. My son Jai was in his tenth grade in one of the best schools in Mumbai. He was an average child in academics but was honest and transparent. He was undergoing a difficult time coping up with his studies. The school was in the usual rat race of maintaining its reputation and was pressurizing Jai to perform better but was not working. He was intelligent but his learning style was different and this was having a strain on both of us. It was in one of the meetings that the school Principal made it clear that Jai would not be able to appear

---

44 https://www.hindustantimes.com/india-news/humility-simplicity-compassion-what-interactions-with-dr-kalam-taught-me/story-PKY8M00kZ5jEgnquiDa2IP.html

for this tenth-grade finals. Together with this news she opened new venues for us which would help Jai to cope up with his difficulties and move ahead in life. I guess she (bless her) suggested the best option possible, for the other one was to change schools. The world suddenly seemed so cruel and the extent to which education was commercialized and made competitive sickened me. She shared with me an experience by one of the other parents, whose son had similar issues and was taken to the United States where he coped up well. She emphasized that it would be a wise decision. I went through the process of checking out, researching, and communicating with concerned people. I started understanding what my child was going through. So going to the United States was indeed a good decision. Now I had to face another hurdle that was convincing the family. Ours was a joint family and communicating was no easy task. Leaving the family and going so far without any firm assurance regarding Jai's future did not go well with the family. I was under tremendous pressure and it was at that time I remembered my Guruji Pramukh Swamiji. He was the only person I had faith in who would do justice and take care of my family members. I wrote to him stating all facts and about our decision to take him to the United States. Within two days I received his reply and it was affirmative. I was overjoyed and felt blessed. The way he had solved my problem would only have been possible by the highest form of spiritual empathy. He knew exactly what was going on my mind and my heart and his blessings conveyed to me, "I was not alone" he was with me all the time. He infused courage and self-confidence and I felt utmost peace in my heart and was assured of the fulfillment of my mission. That day was the most memorable day of my life. He gave me the support I needed at the right time and in the most comforting way. Things went smoothly thereafter. I was so proud when my son finished his high school in Honor roll and received a trophy for being the best all-rounder.

Only spiritually elevated souls exhibit this kind of empathy. True empathy dissolves "I" and "Mine" which is the cause of all misery in life. This narrowness of vision and thought lands us in the field of exclusivity whereas naturally we belong to inclusivity. The basis of Hindu wisdom is our underlying harmony. The world today has turned competitive and this breeds selfishness and envy. The Hindu civilization has always shown us the path towards cooperation.

CHAPTER 3

COOPERATION TRANSCENDS COMPETITION

"Nothing truly valuable can be achieved except by the unselfish co-operation of many individuals"

– Albert Einstein

"We must re-program ourselves to understand that co-operation is higher principle than competition"

– Bryant McGill

I feel competition is inherently destructive. Many things fall into a category where they are most likely not to be worth accepting. They might have a few advantages but with competition it is not true. Our culture is based on harmony, cooperation, and mutual inclusiveness. Almost all fields like business, education, and sports support competition. Since a long period of time, we have been exposed to this kind of life and so it has become natural for us and we accept it as normal. We never pause for a moment to ponder whether some things we have taken for granted are right or wrong. What are the consequences that we would face later? We never question things because our goals are materialistic related to wealth and fame. If we investigate the process, we will find that competition damages our self-esteem and creates anxiety. We stop sharing and caring and become selfish. Failure is not acceptable in competition. We as humans are not made for competition but are finely tuned for cooperation. This leads us to peace and joy because we get connected. Cooperation leads to progress.

Einstein one of the centuries greatest physicists says:

"A human being is part of the whole universe, a part limited in time and space. We experience our self, our thoughts, and feelings as something separate from the rest. A kind of optical illusion of consciousness. This delusion is a kind of prison for us, restricting our personal desires and affection for the few people nearest to us. Our task must be to free ourselves from this prison by widening our circle of compassion to embrace all living creatures and all of nature in its beauty. We shall require a substantially new manner of thinking if mankind is to survive."[45] Alfie Kohn a well-known American author and lecturer in the field of education says that there is good evidence that productivity in the workplace suffers as a result of competition. Research is even more compelling in classroom settings. David Johnson, a professor of social psychology at the University of Minnesota and his colleagues reviewed all studies they could find on the subject from 1924-1980. Sixty-five of the studies

---

45 https://www.goodreads.com/quotes/369-a-human-being-is-a-part-of-the-whole-called

found that children learn better when they work cooperatively as opposed to competitively. Eight found the reverse and thirty-six found no differences. The more complex the learning task, the worse the children fared in a competitive environment.

In a creativity study by Brandeis University psychologist Teresa Amabile, asked the children to make silly collages. Some competed for prizes and some did not. Seven artists independently rated the work. It turned out those who were trying to win produced collages that were much less creative and less spontaneous, complex, and varied than others. Competition breeds hostility. Children envy winners and competition makes it difficult to regard others as potential friends.[46]

Famous philosopher and author Bertrand Russell has rightly said "The only thing that will redeem mankind is cooperation.[47] In his book 'Biology of Belief' the renowned molecular biologist Bruce Lipton says, on one side of the line is the world defined by Neo-Darwinism which casts life as an unending war among battling bio chemical robots. On the other side of the line is the new biology which casts life as a cooperative journey among powerful

---

46 Excerpt from - working mother September 1987 - alfiekohn.org
47 https://www.brainyquote.com/quotes/bertrand_russell_382379

individuals who can program themselves to create joy filled lives.[48]

Competition has sunk so deep down into our lives that we do not realize that we are trapped into its clutches. What is supposed to be inherent in us 'cooperation' is vanishing. We visit different places brimming with beauty such as forests, rivers, mountains, lakes, flora, and fauna belonging to this magnificent place we call Home. This captivating habitat, our mother earth is an epitome of cooperation. If we look with the soul's eye, vibrations, and reflections in the living world all aim at unity or oneness. Wherever we look we observe harmony. Nature is like a huge orchestra, the musicians all playing different instruments but remaining in tune and rhythm with one another under the conductor's guidance. Nothing is out of place and such harmonious music touches one's soul. Competition breeds selfishness. One tends to think about oneself only. Goals must be achieved even at the cost of tossing and jostling others. We become less sensitive to others as the rage within extinguishes the human light. Cooperation is all embracing and generates everlasting peace. Positive vibrations surround it diminishing the negative

---

48 Biology of Belief by Bruce Lipton - Introduction

vibrations leaving the environment healthy and bright. It creates an atmosphere of love and affection which in turn spreads out more goodness and infuses a healing touch all around it. Animosity has no place amidst cooperation, so calmness and peace prevail which purify our mind and heart. A pure heart is the gateway to divinity. Pure and serene thoughts raise our levels of consciousness to make the path towards self-realization materialize which is the purpose and goal of human life. We belong to a glorious culture which is all encompassing and holistic. There is an urgent need for today's youth to reconnect to their traditions and values in order to remain happy and content in life.

CHAPTER 4

HOMEWARD BOUND

> **"If we are to preserve culture, we must continue to create it."**
>
> – *Johan Huizinga*

> **"Traditions are the guideposts driven deep into our sub conscious mind. The most powerful ones are those we can't even describe, aren't even aware of".**
>
> – *Ellen Goodman*

Swami Nikhilanandji of the Chinmayananda mission says, "We the people of India belong to the great ancient Vedic culture. Our culture is to us what the environment and soil are for trees. Trees grow healthiest in an environment native to them. Deeper and stronger their roots, greater the height of their trees. If we have a community that wants to be healthy and at the same time soar to great heights in all fields of human endeavor it is necessary, we remember our culture and be firmly rooted to it."[49]

How many of us would get impacted by the above lines? Few I guess, very few. The effect of colonization has left a deep impression on our psyche

---

49 Pinterest quotes

and post-independence till now little has changed. Britishers have left behind their legacy and have succeeded in wiping out our original way of thinking and living. They have successfully attacked our roots meaning our traditions, customs, rituals, heritage, and languages too. By this I do not mean we have to shut down to all outside ideas, but not at the cost of our culture. Gandhiji has very clearly expressed this idea by saying "I do not want my house to be walled in on all sides and my windows to be stuffed. I want the culture of all lands to be blown into my house as freely as possible. But I refuse to be blown off my feet by any."[50]

Cultural development takes place over a long period of time. Cultural ideas are specific to certain ethnic groups and vary from nation to nation and vary within a nation. India is extremely diverse in its cultural components. The outer aspects of different cultures within the nation vary from region to region but inner most ideals remain the same. This is the reason we say "Unity in Diversity". Culture is also influenced by the physical and social environment. During colonial rule the British succeeded in creating an awe in the minds of Indian people. People started believing in the superiority of their ways of thinking

---

50 https://www.goodreads.com/author/quotes/5810891. Mahatma_Gandhi?page=7

and living. They falsely claimed that whatever was indigenous was primitive and of inferior value. Our ancient Education system of Gurukuls was far more superior and aimed at all round development of the students. Its approach being holistic. The British knew that if this system of Education was replaced with theirs, introducing the English language would help them a lot. A major turn of events took place with the arrival of Lord Babington Macaulay. When he arrived in India the committee of Public Instructions set up by the British was locked five against five members. Five members had opted for education in vernacular languages with English coming at a later stage. The other five members wanted education based on the heritage of its classical languages like Sanskrit, Persian and Arabic. Macaulay, being the president of this committee, wasted no time in introducing English. He believed in the superiority of his civilization. Most British officers at higher administrative levels were arrogant and snobbish. They never tried to understand or experience the beauty and depth of cultural traditions and customs of this beautiful land. Their ego created a sort of mask hiding from view the universal ideals and wisdom, this ancient land had to offer to the world.

Speaking of the English language, I am not against it. Languages are unique and have their own beauty and expression. The problem is that English is not our language and it is foreign. I understand and accept its importance in the global world as a language of communication. In India we have given undue importance to it at the cost of our regional languages. India is home to so many different languages and dialects. These languages are spoken by one sixth of the world's population which is by no means a small number. Language is a very important aspect of culture. Our mother tongue is the closest to our heart. It has a very high emotional value. It belongs to the soil and environment and is connected to the flora and fauna of the land. The air, water and breeze carry the pulse of the language and are a great unifying factor. It encourages freedom of thought and unleashes creativity to its fullest potential, the capability to harmonize. Research proves that if early education is imparted in the mother tongue it ensures a sound foundation with clarity of thought and expression. It is a false belief that if a child is tutored in its mother tongue, then later English language becomes difficult to grasp. There are examples of quite a few brilliant outstanding Indians who in the past and near past have proven the above idea wrong. Rabindranath Tagore studied in Bengali and went on to learn the English language. He received the Nobel prize in literature for his poem 'Geetanjali.' If the translation had such a powerful effect, then we can guess how magnificent the original poem in Bengali would be. Mahatma Gandhi too was educated in Gujarati and rose to become a brilliant Barrister. His works are written in impeccable English. Other great intellectuals were Sardar Patel, Dr. Kalam, Dr. Ambedkar, Dr Radhakrishnan, Dr Rajagopalachari, Tilak and many more. These are examples of outstanding Indians who have contributed immensely to the nation. There are Indian people in different fields of endeavor who have done exceptionally well nationally and internationally despite their basic schooling in their mother tongue.

Mahatma Gandhi said, "It is my considered opinion that the English language in the manner it has been given emasculated the English educated Indians. It has put serious strain upon the Indian student's nervous energy and has made us imitators. The process of displacing our vernaculars has been one of the saddest chapters in British connection. Ram Mohan Rai would have been a great reformer and Lokmanya Tilak would have been a greater scholar if they had not started with the handicap of having to think in English and transmit their thoughts chiefly in English. Their effect on their own people is marvelous as it would have been greater if they had been brought up under a less unnatural system. No doubt they both gained from their knowledge of rich treasures of English literature, but these should have been accessible to them through their own vernaculars. No country can become a nation by producing a race of imitators. Think of what would have happened to the English if they had not an authorized version of bible. I do believe that Chaitanya, Kabir, Nanak, Guru Gobind Singh, Shivaji, and Pratap were greater men than Ram Mohan Rai and Tilak. I know comparisons are odious. All are equally great in their own way but judge by the results the effects of Ram Mohan Rai and Tilak on masses is not so permanent or far reaching as that of the others more fortunately born. Judged by the obstacles they had to surmount they were giants and both would have been greater in achieving results if they had not been handicapped by the system under which they received training. I refuse to believe that Raja and Tilak would not have thoughts they did without the knowledge of English language. Of all the superstitions that affect India none is so great as that a knowledge of English language is necessary for imbibing ideas of liberty and developing accuracy of thoughts. It should be remembered there has been only one system of education before the county for the past fifty years. Only one medium of expression forced upon the country, we have therefore no data before us as to what would have been but for the education in the existing schools and colleges. This however we do know that India is poorer than fifty years ago, less able to defend herself and her children have less stamina. I need not be told that this is due to defect in system of government. The system of education is its most defective part. It was conceived and born in error for English rulers honestly believed the indigenous system to be worse than useless. It has been nurtured in sin for the tendency has been to dwarf the Indian body mind and soul.[51]

Gandhiji was so right that seventy-five years after independence we have worsened. We are progressing at a very fast pace in the direction of amnesia regarding our roots, culture, and traditions. We take pride when our young children recite nursery rhymes and speak in English language. Have we ever sat down and tried to make sense of what these rhymes are? They make no sense for there is no connection to this land and culture. Of course, they appear alien. Our education system is becoming more and more commercialized. Introduction of the English education system in guise of benevolent exteriors is posing dangers towards whom we are oblivious. I am not totally against this system which has its own benefits but my concern is it is at the cost of our native languages. This system of education has replaced our traditional and original way of learning

---

51 https://www.mkgandhi.org/towrds_edu/chap02.htm

causing alienation from our indigenous knowledge modes. Sending children to such high-end schools have become a sort of social status symbol among the elites. We all need to awaken and introspect deeply as to where we stand and what honest measures should we take to rectify this. Every new idea comes with its advantages and disadvantages. It is the same with globalization. We are losing our identities and trying to become copies of one another. Our morals and values are at an all-time low exposing us to dangers, pushing us into a deep chasm of deception. To express one's unique identity in this era of globalization there arises a need for real courage. We need to remain who and what we are, proudly retaining our heritage and traditions. If we remain sensitive and contribute positively to global progress and peace, I do not see why we should feel uncomfortable being different! Our ancient wisdom tells us that the purpose of human life is to evolve spiritually and expand our consciousness. Our proud lineage goes back to Rishis and Saints. There is a beautiful description of the same by Rabindranath Tagore. He says "The rishis who have attained the supreme soul in knowledge were filled with wisdom and having found Him in union with the soul were in perfect harmony with inner self, they having realized Him in heart were free from all selfish desires and having experienced Him in all activities for the world had attained calmness. The Rishis were they who having reached the supreme God from all sides had found abiding peace had become united with all, had entered the life of the universe."[52]

These great Rishi's were blessed ones for to them were revealed the oldest scriptures known to men, 'The Vedas'. Veda Vyas the giant amongst sages was responsible for compiling and classifying the Vedas. He also authored 'The Puranas,' the last of which is the famous Bhagwat Purana. The essence of all scriptures lies in a Shloka written by Veda Vyas.

आलोऽयसर्वशास्त्राणि विचार्यैवं पुनः पुनः ।
इदमेकं सुनिष्पन्न ध्येयो नारायणो हरिः ।। 78

After studying all the scriptures in depth, I thought over and again and came to only one conclusion: that the purpose and goal of human life is to seek God.

---

[52] https://www.speakingtree.in/blog/the-relation-of-the-individual-to-the-universe-7

CHAPTER 5

VEDAS: THE GATEWAY TO DIVINITY

By William Dwight Whitney

Antidote

ऋचो अक्षरे परमे व्योमन्यस्मिन्देवा अधि विश्वे निषेदुः ।
यस्तं न वेद किमृचा करिष्यति य इत्तद्विदुस्त इमे समासते ॥

Richo Akshare parame vyoman yasmin Deva adhi vishve nisheduḥ yastanna veda kim richa karishyati ya ittadvidus ta ime samāsate

The verses of the Veda exist in the collapse of fullness (the kshara of 'A') in the transcendental field, the self, in which reside all the Devas, the impulses of creative intelligence, and the Laws of Nature responsible for the whole manifest universe. He whose awareness is not open to this field, what can the verses accomplish for him? Those who know this level of reality are established in evenness wholeness of life. (Rig Veda 1.164.39)

The Vedas are indeed direct revelations to these great rishis when in a state of inspiration. These revelations were true to them as much as our sensory perceptions are true to us. The sages experienced this truth which was passed down to disciples in oral traditions. Veda Vyas divided the Veda into four parts: Rig Veda, Yajur Veda, Sama Veda and Atharva Veda. Each Veda had four parts: Samhita, Brahmana, Aranyaka and Upanishads.

The Rig Veda Samhita is in "Rik" form or Hymn. It has ten books or Mandalas. Each Mandala consists of

Hymns of Suktas (Well recited) intended for various rituals. The Suktas in turn consist of individual stanzas called "Rik" (Praise) which are further analyzed into units of verse called "Pada" (step). More than the letters, the sounds are important. It is that frequency which connects to the frequency of the Cosmos. The meters mostly used in case of Rik are Gayatri, Anushtubh, Trisubh and Jagati. The Rig Vedic hymns are dedicated to various deities chief being, Indra, Agni and Soma. Also invoked are Surya, Vayu, Ashwins and Rivers mainly Saptasindhu and Saraswati. Brahmanas are commentaries or explanations on Vedic rituals. Rig Veda has two Brahmanas "Aitareya" and "Kaushtaki". Aranyaka discuss proper performance of rituals and were meant for Vanaprastha or forest dwellers. Rig Veda has two Aranyaka, Rig Veda Aranyaka and Kaushtaki Aranyaka. They contain the philosophy behind ritual sacrifice in Vedas. Aranyaka describes and discusses rituals from various perspectives but some include philosophical speculations. The content of Aranyaka is somewhere in transition between ritualism and meta ritualistic point of view. It shows movement towards abstract philosophical thoughts which mature completely in the Upanishads.[53] Rig Veda has one Upanishad the Aitareya Upanishad.

---

53 https://www.newworldencyclopedia.org/

Yajur Veda comes from the root word in Sanskrit, 'Yaj' meaning to worship. It is the Veda primarily of the prose mantra for worship rituals, the 'Yagnas'. Yajur Veda has two branches Krishna Yajur Veda and Shukla Yajur Veda. The Samhita contains 1875 verses built on the foundation of Rig Veda verses. It has one Brahmana named the Shatpatha Brahmana meaning one hundred paths. It contains opinions on rituals. The Shukla Yajur Veda has one Aranyaka called "Brihadaranyaka" and Krishna Yajur Veda has three Aranyakas named "Taittiriya, Maitrayana and Katha" and it has six Upanishads "Brihadaranyaka Upanishad, Isopanishad, Taittiriya Upanishad, Kathopanishad and Shvetashvatara Upanishad and Maitrayaniya Upanishad.[54]

The third Veda is Samaveda, Saman meaning 'song' it consists of 1549 verses. Except 75 verses rest are taken from Rig Veda, the purpose of Sama Veda was Liturgical (Public Worship). Samaveda Samhita is meant to be sung and not read. It has two brahmanas, the Panchavimsa and Jaiminiya. Samaveda has one Aranyaka named Talavakara and two Upanishads Kena and Chhandogya. Indian classical music and dance are rooted in Samaveda. Sama Veda also mentions instruments.[55]

---

54 https://vedicheritage.gov.in/
55 https://vedicheritage.gov.in/

The last Veda is Atharva Veda. It may be named after Rishis Atharvana who composed mantras to counteract diseases. It is the knowledge store house of Atharvanas that has procedures for everyday life. It contains 730 hymns, 6000 mantras and 20 kangas. One sixth of the verses are from Rig Veda hymns pertaining to recovery from illness, surgical and medical treatment and remedy from medicinal herbs and hymns for peace. It contains one Brahmana called "Gopatha Brahmana". The three Upanishads within the Atharva Veda are Mundaka, Mandukya and Prashana.[56]

The Upanishads come towards the end of the Vedas. In general, the Vedas are divided into two parts - Karma Kanda (Ritual) and Gyan Kanda (Knowledge). They are included in Shruti literature meaning they were not written but revealed. They contain the difficult discussions of ultimate philosophical questions. They are also known as Rahasya Grantha. About 108 Upanishads exist and are listed in Muktikopanishad. These are divided among the four Vedas.

10 from Rigveda | 19 from Shukla Yajurveda | 32 from Krishna Yajurveda | 16 from Samaveda | 31 from Atharvaveda.

---

56 https://vedicheritage.gov.in/

They represent the knowledge of Brahman. So also known as Brahmavidya. They investigate the ultimate nature of reality. The main subject matter of all the Upanishads is the same but the method of investigation or enquiry is different. All of them point to the same ultimate goal. The Upanishads together with Brahma Sutras and Bhagavad Gita are considered as the highest authority based on which different systems of Philosophy in India are based.

Many Indians perform rituals every day whether out of faith or because they are compelled to do so. More and more young educated Indians are uneasy with the concept of rituals. Some of them also coin it superstitious. The sad part is that we have disconnected ourselves from a very important and essential aspect of our tradition without delving deeper to seek truth. Rituals were very important in Vedic times and they lost importance for some time and surfaced again with the advent of Bhakti movement. Adi Shankara was one of the stalwarts responsible for revival of Sanatana Dharma based on Vedas. Starting from South India the Bhakti movement travelled Northwards. A ritual when performed keeping in mind the underlying meaning has the power to affect our mind and consciousness. The purpose behind rituals is to align energies of self with that of the cosmos to bring in desired results for expansion of our consciousness. We have seen many times how isolated tribes alienated from the modern world survive by remaining in contact with the cosmos through different rituals. They derive their life force directly from the cosmos. The changing seasons, movement of planets, lunar cycles have a subtle effect on us. Rituals help us to maintain a conscious awareness of the universal laws of nature (Ruta). Sanatan Hindu Dharma states that the universe is a Macrocosm and the human body is a Microcosm. The Vedic mantras keep in synchronization the microcosm and the macrocosm. All that exists in the universe exists subtly in our body too. We have these connections with the universe but have been desensitized beyond hope. We need a paradigm shift in our way of thinking to be able to reconnect with the universe. Our ideals of faith and conscience are drowned beneath the waters of logic and reason. We need to resurface again. The secret of unlocking this immortal treasure box lies in the Vedas and other scriptures.

CHAPTER 6

UPANISHADS: THE KNOWLEDGE DIVINE

Swami Vivekananda said, "The human thoughts reached Himalayan peaks in Upanishads." Upanishad means sitting near the master. The style of Upanishads is in form of dialogue between master and disciple. In some places names are mentioned and some places they are not. The central theme of Upanishads is monotheism. The fundamental principle is that the universe is pervaded by the energy of the supreme cosmic being. The Upanishads have their own unique style wherein we find dialogues, narrations, episodes, similes, metaphors, allegory, and symbolism. The Upanishadic knowledge is transcendent meaning not bound by time and space. It is relevant in today's time and in it we find the quest for eternal truth. According to Swami Vivekananda in this Enquiry the element of fearlessness is very prominent.

A long time ago Alexander the Great was stranded on the banks of the great river Indus deep in conversation with Dandi Sanyasi. He was impressed by his wisdom and invited him to Greece. The Fakir refused and Alexander became tough and threatened to kill him but the Fakir was unmoved. He said "Do not pile empty threats on me. I am the immortal soul; I am not born nor will I die. How can you kill me?" This kind of boldness is reflected frequently in the Upanishads. The Upanishadic knowledge is so powerful and full of insights that it has had a mesmerizing effect on people all around the world. Arthur Schopenhauer the famous German philosopher, Emerson, Thoreau the great American Transcendental Authors and many great Physicists remained in awe of Upanishadic wisdom. The Upanishads say "When a man dies what does not leave him? The voice of the dead man goes into fire, his breath in wind, his mind into moon, his hearing into quarters of heaven, his body into earth and spirit into space. Those wise ones who see that the consciousness within them is the same consciousness within all living beings attain peace. (Kathopnishad)

The Upanishads help us in lifting the envelope of ignorance which is masking eternal truth. Embedded within the fabric of Upanishad is the message portraying futility of worldly possessions, titles, wealth, fame and more. The purpose of human life is spiritual evolution. Human beings have been endowed with special faculties which are to be used in expansion of consciousness. There is an inherent inclination for spiritual quest within us all. It lies in deep slumber unless awakened. The glitter and glamour of materialism shrouds this eternal truth. We are not mere physical bodies but are spiritual beings with physical bodies. Our 'Atman' (soul) is our real self. It is ever blissful and immortal (Sat, Chit, Ananda). The Bhagwat Gita states this beautifully in Chapter 2 shloka 23

नैनं छिन्दन्ति शस्त्राणि नैनं दहति पावकः ।
न चैनं क्लेदयन्त्यापो न शोषयति मारुतः ।।

Weapons cannot shred the soul, nor can fire burn it. Water cannot wet it, nor can the wind dry it. The soul is eternal, never is it born nor does it die.

Lofty ideals and profound truths emerge out of the Upanishads having power to lift one and all into divine realms in which none of the materialistic pleasures exist but a place and state of spiritual bliss which is beyond the grasp of Earthly forms. Spiritual gains can never be valued in material terms. One must have faith in it to experience this, Bliss.

The central lesson of the Upanishad points to the single truth that every being in this universe is pervaded by a supreme divine energy and that is the ultimate reality. Upanishads explain that it is possible to transcend both intellect and senses. They teach self-control and sacrifice. Certain truths in the Upanishads are not expressed directly but revealed through implied meaning. Therefore, a Guru is necessary for decoding. The term 'Upanishad' 'itself means "sitting near a Guru." When one attains the knowledge of self and realizes his oneness with Paramatma and remains in obedience to that wisdom there is no room for fear, insecurity, sorrow nor cycles of birth and death. This is the ultimate liberation or Moksh. The mantras of the Upanishad are very difficult to grasp and so at the pious feet of our Guru we must surrender for his grace, to develop a thought process to purify our minds and sense organs. Only then in such a mind the knowledge of the Upanishads reveals itself. It is not within my ability or capacity to write on the Upanishads. Many great scholars and saints have written commentaries on the Upanishads. It is difficult for a layman to grasp the meaning or wholly comprehend the complex mantras. So, I offer my sincere humble prostrations at the lotus feet of my Gurus HDH Pramukh Swamiji and HDH Mahant Swamiji whose lives have been the epitome of essence of the Upanishads. Their lives have been a source of constant inspiration to millions to live in accordance with the sacred ideals of our holy scriptures which include the Upanishads. Keeping this in mind I have tried to take stories from Upanishads and elaborate on their deeper meaning and practical application in everyday life. Anybody who wishes to delve deeper into these divine mysteries can always look for more literature which is easily available.

Aitareya Upanishad (Rig Veda)

It is encompassed within the Aitareya Aranyaka of Rig Veda and so is named Aitareya Upanishad. It contains three chapters and is one of the older Upanishads, it deals with metaphysical questions on the creation of the universe and its creator (Paramatma). It discusses in length the creation of the human body and how the soul enters the physical body and becomes subject to hunger and thirst. It also describes how innumerable embodied souls undergo numerous cycles of birth and death and in the end become wise and attain liberation. It identifies consciousness as the first cause of creation meaning the basis of the universe is consciousness. The third chapter instructs us to perform Upasana of Paramatma together with knowledge of his greatness.

Upanishads of Yajurveda
Brihadaranyaka Upanishad

It belongs to Shukla Yajur Veda. It is enclosed within the Vajanaseyi Brahmana of Shukla Yajur Veda 'Brihad' means 'large' and it was contemplated in a forest and so was called Aranyaka. The famous story of Yajnavalkya Rishi and his wife Maitreyi is found in this text. Yajnavalkya was well known for his wisdom and intellect. As he entered the Vanprasthashram stage in life, he decided to renounce home and retire to forest. He decided to inform his two wives Maitreyi and Katyayani regarding his decision. He had planned to divide his worldly possessions between his two wives so that they would live peacefully. Maitreyi was suddenly pensive and asked her husband if all this wealth would make her immortal? The Rishi said that it was not possible. So Maitreyi asked Yagnavalkya, how these worldly possessions would help her? He explained to her that his wealth would only sustain her in this world but would not buy her immortality. So Maitreyi told her husband that she was not interested in material wealth as it would cause more bondage. She was very intelligent and asked Yagnavalkya the reason why he was renouncing this wealth and moving out to the forest. To this the Rishi beautifully explained to her that the happiness and joy that everyone experiences is because of the presence of all pervading Paramatma dwelling inside all. The rishi then told her that he was leaving for the forest in order to contemplate on the supreme being (Paramatma) and move ahead on the path of enlightenment. He had fulfilled his duties as a householder and that now was the time for him to enter the Vanaprastha ashrama. Maitreyi decided to choose the difficult path forsaking luxuries and accompanied the Rishi to the forest.

The story of king Janaka and Rishi Yajnavalkya.

There was a king named Janaka of Videha. He once performed Bahudakshinaka Yagna. A great number of brahmins and scholars had gathered to attend this, Yagna. The king asked, "Who is the wisest amongst you all? I have one thousand cows and each cow has ten gold coins on each horn so whoever is the wisest, one who is Brahmanishta (one who knows brahman) can take away these cows. Yagnavalkya called out to his disciple Samashrava and commended him to lead away these cows to his ashram. The Brahmins became jealous and objected to this. They said he had to undergo a test to prove himself. Yagnavalkya responded saying that he needed the cows so was leading them away. The Brahmins rose to challenge him. Yagnavalkya accepted the challenge. One by one the Brahmins asked questions which were immediately answered by Yagnavalkya. The Brahmins questioned regarding realization of Atma and Paramatma. He answered them unflinchingly. The Brahmins were aghast and did not know what to do. To everyone's amazement a Rishika named Gargi Vachaknavi stood up and asked difficult questions to which she received prompt answers. She also gave up and sat down. Yagnavalkya was declared victorious and received all the 1000 cows. We find here in the Upanishads the system of debating and discussions on the questions raised by the scholars. This way the knowledge was shared and new horizons regarding different aspects opened. There was also a lot of clarity on issues which were difficult to comprehend. In this way there was lot of sharing and transfer of knowledge as the scholars used to come from different places. So, we come to know that ancient India had always been a seat of learning and we always believed in enquiry. The following are the two mantras from Bruhadaranyaka Upanishad.

असतो मा सद्गमय ।
तमसो मा ज्योतिर्गमय ।
मृत्योर्मा अमृतं गमय ।
ॐ शान्तिः शान्तिः शान्तिः ॥

Meaning:

1. Om, (O Lord) Keep me not in (the Phenomenal World of) Unreality, but make me go towards the Reality (of Eternal Self),
2. Keep me not in (the Ignorant State of) Darkness, but make me go towards the Light (of Spiritual Knowledge),
3. Keep me not in (the World of) Mortality, but make me go towards the World of Immortality (of Self-Realization),
4. Om, Peace, Peace, Peace.[57]

ॐ पूर्णमदः पूर्णमिदं पूर्णात्पूर्णमुदच्यते ।
पूर्णस्य पूर्णमादाय पूर्णमेवावशिष्यते ॥
ॐ शान्तिः शान्तिः शान्तिः ॥

Meaning:

1. Om, that (Outer World) is Purna (Full with Divine Consciousness); This (Inner World) is also Purna

---

[57] https://greenmesg.org/stotras/vedas/om_asato_ma_sadgamaya.php

(Full with Divine Consciousness); From Purna is manifested Purna (From the Fullness of Divine Consciousness the World is manifested),

2. Taking Purna from Purna, Purna indeed remains (Because Divine Consciousness is Non-Dual and Infinite),
3. Om, Peace, Peace, Peace.[58]

Isha Upanishad

This Upanishad is one of the smallest Upanishads in the last (40th) chapter of the Samhita of Shukla Yajur Veda. Maximum number of commentaries have been written on this Upanishad which itself reflects that it is filled with spiritual wisdom. We might ponder as to what is in it which has led many wise and deep thinkers to introspect within and then pen down these wonderful ideas on paper to arouse the maximum good in all those who read it.

Mahatma Gandhi once said that "If all our history and culture including all sacred scripture were to perish living behind no clue and suddenly one day if someone gets hold of a small piece of paper where in it is written the first Mantra of Isha Upanishad everything will revive, such is the power and influence of this Mantra.

---

[58] https://greenmesg.org/stotras/vedas/om_purnamadah_purnamidam.php

ईशा वास्यमिदं सर्वं यत्किञ्च जगत्यां जगत्।
तेन त्यक्तेन भुञ्जीथा मा गृधः कस्यस्विद्धनम् ॥

The whole world is pervaded by supreme being and so everything belongs to Him. One should only accept things necessary for oneself and not others knowing well whom they belong to. Do not covet others wealth.

If this one mantra is understood exactly in the way it is meant to be, the world would get rid of all problems facing mankind today. Perception for this is needed at individual level and group level where intellectuals and world leaders meet to discuss and solve burning issues. If we develop faith in the Ishavasya concept our sense of doer ship, our pride, our prejudices, judgmental actions, and much more will vanish. The walls, boundaries, and barriers we create result in divisions causing hatred, envy, anger, and all of these will crumble down. Our claims on land, water, and forest of this beautiful planet will stand nullified. We will be able to live a life ever blissful surrounded by a vast diverse landscape appearing distinct at a material level but unified at abstract level. I would call it the quantum level. The creator envelopes all animate and inanimate things in this world. The same consciousness pervades in all beings indicating unity and harmony cancelling out scope for war, competition, and hatred.

The Isha Upanishad gives us four important instructions:

1. Creator pervades whole creation
2. Karmayoga that is performance of one's duty.
3. Importance of Knowledge together with Karma.
4. Prayers to the supreme Entity.

We should live with an awareness that God is supreme and all pervading. Since God is the true controller of this universe, we should perform our karmas without desire for results. We must be aware of karmas which hurt us spiritually. Cultivating in our minds the sense for discrimination between truth and untruth mentioned as Vidya and Avidya in the Upanishad. Lastly the Upanishad ends with prayers urging us to remain positive and focused on Paramatma. It teaches us to live a balanced life wherein we fulfill our worldly duties without forgetting our spiritual progress.[59]

Taittiriya Upanishad

It is encompassed within Krishna Yajurveda and is recited as a part of Taittiriya Aranyaka. The Upanishad include verses that are partly prayers and benedictions and partly instructions on phonetics

---

59 https://www.swami-krishnananda.org/

and praxis, partly advice on ethics and morals given to graduating students from Vedic Gurukuls. It also contains Philosophical instructions. The Upanishad has three chapters or Vallis. The first being Shiksha Valli, Shiksha meaning instruction of education. As the name suggests it is related to education of students starting from initiating into schools through responsibilities while in school and after graduation. It also includes hints of self-knowledge. One of the important concepts in education was mastering principles of sound where structure, vowels, consonants, balancing (stress, meter) correct pronunciation and connection of sounds in a word. This was of utmost importance for oral preservation of Vedas in their original forms when transmitted from generation to generation. Concepts pertaining to ethics were also taught to the students. In the end the teacher imparted to the students' golden rules to live life based on morality and ethics. Some of the teachings are as follows:

> Never err from truth
> Never err from Dharma
> Never neglect your wellbeing
> Never neglect your prosperity
> Never neglect Swadhyaya

Antidote

मातृ देवो भव ।
पितृ देवो भव ।
आचार्य देवो भव ।
अतिथि देवो भव ॥

Honour thy mother as God.
Honour thy Father as God.
Honour thy Teacher as God.
Honour thy Guest as God.

Let your actions be uncensorable none else those acts that you consider good when done to you do those to others none else. (T.U.1.11.2)

The second chapter or Valli is Anand Valli the name itself suggests 'Ananda' meaning 'Bliss' the supreme being or the Paramatma is blissful and so root of all bliss is Paramatma. This divine bliss cannot be compared to our material happiness. It is infinite bliss and cannot be measured but for the sake of understanding the verse starts with bliss experienced by one man and this man being complete in sense of physical, mental and wealth attributes, then goes further up in the realm of devas where we find more happiness and then further up till the bliss of Paramatma which is beyond our grasp. To attain the all-blissful Paramatma is the essence of this chapter. This being the goal of every spiritual aspirant. The third chapter is Bhrigu Valli. It is so named because

Brigu Rishi became his father's disciple and through him received the knowledge of all blissful Paramatma.

Here in Tattiriya Upanishad we see a unique combination of Aparavidya that is the worldly knowledge which we saw in the first Valli that is Shiksha Valli and then Para vidya (Spiritual) in the last two vallis namely Anand Valli and Brigu Valli where the true goal of human life has been explained. We find in the Vedic era an integrated approach to all round development of an individual for the rishis knew very well that a spiritually mature individual will always succeed in the material world, and so the emphasis was laid on spiritual knowledge together with worldly knowledge.[60]

Katha Upanishad

It belongs to the Katha branch of Krishna Yajurveda. Katha Upanishad is regarded as the best amongst the Upanishads by many scholars. It is my view that this Upanishad is very clear in explaining Brahma vidya. It begins with a description of Vishwajeet Yagna performed by a Brahmin named Vajashravas. Yagnas used to be performed to please the devas in

---

60   https://www.vyasaonline.com/

return for worldly gains. Here we see a subtle but very clear transition from ritualism to spiritualism as we move further down the Upanishad. The yagnas symbolize "Ritualism" and were performed with utmost precision in chanting as well as laying of the sacred altar (yagna Kund). Vajashravas after performing the yagna was donating cows as per the usual custom. These cows were old and of no use. And so, his son Nachiketa questioned his father regarding this, but received no answer. Nachiketa was persistent, a quality which angered his father but pleased lord Yama as we will see further down in the Upanishad. When he did not get the appropriate response from his father, he did not give up but asked his father as to whom he would give away himself. His father in anger shouted, "To death I give thee." So, without even losing a moment Nachiketa walked away to the abode of Lord Yama (God of Death). There he stood for three days and three nights without food and water as Lord Yama was not there. When Lord Yama returned, he found this young boy standing at his door hungry and thirsty but his will and determination steadfast. Lord Yama was saddened at his shortcoming about fulfilling Athithi Dharma so he offered Nachiketa three boons. Thereafter began the dialogue between Lord of Death and Nachiketa spanning across 120 shlokas. It is a treatise addressing victory over death. Scanning down our cultural history we find that Lord Yama has bowed down in front of only two persons, the first being Savitri who brought her husband Satyavan back from abode of death and second Nachiketa to whom Lord Yama revealed the esoteric doctrine of victory over death and then sent him back to this world.

The first boon Nachiketa asked was that his father would let go of his anger, cool down and accept him back lovingly. Lord Yama agrees to this request immediately. For the second boon, Nachiketa requests Lord Yama to instruct him regarding the divine knowledge with which one attains heaven after death. Yama was pleased with his request and taught him the same. He conveyed to Nachiketa that now onward this knowledge would be named after him as Nachiketa Agnividya.

Nachiketa was wise for his age and he demonstrated unbelievable maturity in asking boons. For the third boon, Nachiketa requested Yama to reveal to him the secret knowledge of life after death, the doctrine of immortality. Lord Yama was astonished as he did not expect this. Secretly he was very pleased with Nachiketa but first tried in many ways to dissuade him from asking this boon. He told Nachiketa that the knowledge was very complex and could not be comprehended by the devas and one had to be eligible to be able to receive this knowledge. He tempted Nachiketa to ask for something else but Nachiketa remained firm in his resolve. Yama tried to bribe him with worldly possessions, comforts, precious Jewels, horses, elephants, Apsaras but Nachiketa remained unmoved. Yama tried to lure him on to the path of "Preya" that is progress in worldly affairs leading to wealth, fame and prosperity. Nachiketa was no ordinary child and was made of rare substance. He did not budge till Lord Yama relented and revealed before him the path of "Shreya" to transcend this material world into the realm of the divine. By choosing the path of Shreya one is elevated to a point of no return. One rises above the dualities of life and death. The process and journey being extremely difficult is not meant for the feeble hearted, says Katha Upanishad. So how does one walk this path?

उतिष्ठत जाग्रत प्राप्य वरान्निबोधत, ।
क्षुरासन्न धारा निशिता दुरत्यद्दुर्गम पथः तत् कवयो वदन्ति ।।

Arise! Awake! Approach the great and learn.
Like the sharp edge of a razor is that path,
so, the wise say—hard to tread
and difficult to cross.

I feel this is the central theme of this Upanishad, so powerful and far reaching that it can awaken us out of deepest slumber and inspire us to reach our goal. So ends the story of young Nachiketa. Swami Vivekanand was much influenced by this story that he used to say. "Give me a hundred Nachiketas and I will change the face of the world."

Chhandogya Upanishad

Chhandogya Upanishad is embedded in the Chhandogya Brahmana of Sama Veda. It is one of the oldest Upanishads and is very large. The name is derived from the word "Chanda" which means poetic meter. It has eight chapters each with varying numbers of verses. Klaus Witz in his book "The supreme wisdom of Upanishads" structurally divided Chhandogya Upanishad into three natural groups. The first group largely deals with structure, Stress and rhythmic aspects of language and its expression (speech) particularly with the syllable "AUM." The second group consists of collections on concepts of the universe, life, mind, and spirituality. The third group deals with metaphysical questions on the nature of reality and soul. Certain mantras are allegorical and so the real meaning is hidden. Only an enlightened Guru can read between the lines and explain what the mantras want to reveal. In almost all Upanishads there is a dialogue between the Master and the Seeker in the form of a Disciple. Within the dialogue unfolds the secret doctrine or knowledge meant only for deserving Disciples, the ones who have the intellectual capacity, intuition, and faith to assimilate this esoteric knowledge of Atma and Paramatma called Brahma Vidya. One popular story in Chhandogya Upanishad is about Satyakama Jabala. Satyakama asked his mother regarding his lineage as he wished to be initiated as a disciple under a Guru. His mother Jabala was truthful and told him that she did now know about it as she attended many as a maid servant. She said, "My name is Jabala and yours is Satyakama so you are Satyakama Jabala. Hearing this he went to Gautam rishi's ashram and was asked about his lineage to which he answered truthfully. Gautam rishi was very pleased with his honesty and initiated him as his disciple. The rishi selected four hundred cows and commanded Satyakam to take them away for grazing and return only after the numbers reached One Thousand. Satyakam immediately obeyed his Guru and walked away with the cows. If we think about the task allocated to Satyakam it would seem impossible. What about the time frame? This shows that the Upanishad era youth was made up of rare substance. His mental stability and unwavering faith in his Guru were incredible. The rishis were responsible for transmission of this divine knowledge from generation to generation and had to be very careful in selecting and initiating Disciples.

These Disciples in return were protectors of this knowledge who later transmitted this knowledge to others. They had to endure extremely difficult tasks commanded by their gurus which tested their intellect, Patience, Power of observation, Retention, Virtue of Humility, Aptitude and Reverence for the Gurus. It was no easy task. A certain level of internal development was necessary for receiving this knowledge. If the parents themselves were shining examples, then only would it show in the subsequent generation. This was the reason why sages inquired about the students' lineage before accepting them.

Coming back to Satyakama he wandered with his herd and tended them well. At last, the day dawned when his count reached One Thousand. The Upanishad says that one of the bulls in the herd spoke to Satyakama, "Let us head back to the ashram" Satyakama agreed and started walking back and on his way the bull revealed one quarter of the Brahma Vidya to Satyakama and further stated that the next quarter would be revealed to him by Agni and then the next quarter by the Swan and the last quarter by the Waterfowl. Here we find the use of symbolism where Vayu Deva assumes the form of the Bull, Agni that of Fire, Brahma that of Swan and Varuna as the Waterfowl. The Devas this way imparted the knowledge of Brahman to Satyakama. This was possible only by the grace of his guru Gautam Rishi.

The other story in this Upanishad is about Sage Narada. He approaches Sanatkumar to gain knowledge of Self. So, Sanatkumar questions Narada regarding what all knowledge he had gained till then. Narada has a big list in reply as he is proficient in four Vedas, History, Puranas, Science of Numbers, Logic, Ethics, Politics, Astronomy, Fine Arts and more. Here we realize that the sages were well versed in worldly knowledge too. Now Sanatkumar drops a bombshell telling Narada that all the knowledge he has acquired all these years is just namesake. So, Narada asked Sanatkumar if there was anything greater than namesake to which the wise sage replied 'Speech.' Speech makes everything known so it is greater than Name. Now Narada moves ahead and enquired if there was anything greater than Speech to which Sanatkumar replied 'Mind'. Mind holds both name and speech. Determination or Will is greater than Mind because when one determines one Reflects, one utters Speech and utters Name. Thought is greater than Determination because one Thinks, one Reflects, one utters Speech and one utters Name. Contemplation is greater than thought. Contemplation changes the quality of Thought. Wisdom is greater than Contemplation (Understanding). This deeper understanding is called 'Vignanam'. Strength is greater than Wisdom. A man of deep inner spiritual strength can cause a hundred men of understanding to tremble. This is not mere physical strength. Nourishment is greater than Strength. Water is greater than Nourishment. Nourishment represents the element Earth, so if Water is scarce then Food is scarce. Fire is greater than water for Fire creates water. Space (ether) is greater than Fire. Everything is contained in space. Memory is greater than Space. If there is no Memory, one cannot hear, cannot think, or cannot understand. Hope (aspiration) is greater than Memory. Hope kindles Memory and then Memory learns (aspiration - one must really want God in order to realize). Prime breath (life breath) is greater than Hope because Breath moves as initiated by Prime Breath. At this point Narad seems to be satisfied and does not ask further. Now, the master lifts him from the empirical realm into metaphysical realm and talks about Truth. Narada wants to understand the Truth. When one understands then he speaks the Truth. When one thinks, then only he understands. So, Narada wants to understand Thinking. Sanatkumar says when one has Faith then he Thinks. And when one has firm unwavering Steadfastness (Nishtha) he has Faith. When one is active, one has Steadfastness and when one obtains Happiness, one is Active. Sanatkumar then instructs him about the concept of Happiness. There is no Happiness in finite things, Happiness is in the infinite that is 'Bhooma' or Paramatma.' Infinite is based on its own greatness.

And that infinite is everywhere. It is above you, below you, around you and behind you. Sanatkumar tells Narad that he should realize this Bhooma meaning the 'greatest' (Paramatma). So, this knowledge is called 'Bhuma Vidya'. Sage Narada was competent in 64 fields of knowledge and yet unhappy, he experienced a vacuum in life and felt something amiss. The purpose of life was unfulfilled so peace evaded him and therefore he sought help of the great guru Sanatkumar who was also his elder brother. Sanatkumar lifted Narada from knower of names to the infinite through different levels. Each level being more complex and ironically subtler. Here we can see a gradual movement from the mundane realm into the spiritual realm. Sanatkumar instructed him regarding each level and what it meant. After Narada comprehended and imbibed whatever was taught, he transcended that level and entered the next level till he reached the infinite or the supreme being thus ending the dialogue.[61]

Kena Upanishad

Kena Upanishad belongs to the Talavakara Brahmana of Sama Veda. Kena literally means "By whom" hence it is called Kena Upanishad. This Upanishad is in the

---

61 https://www.sivanandaonline.org//?cmd=displaysection&section_id=588

form of a guru disciple's dialogue and spread over four parts or khandas with a total of 35 mantras. A Disciple asks his Guru questions regarding working of mind and five sense organs, five organs of knowledge and who breaths Prana (life breath) into our life? Who sustains life? The Guru says Paramatma is all doer and he being the supreme sustains life. The fact that Paramatma supports life in the universe is illustrated very beautifully by a story. Once there was a war between Devas and Asuras. By the grace of Paramatma, the Devas won the war. They rejoiced in this victory and became arrogant and boastful and forgot about Paramatma. So, to teach them a lesson He took the form of a Yaksha and went to the Devas. The Devas saw Him but could not recognize who he was so Indra sent Agni Deva to inquire. Yaksha asked Agni Deva for his introduction and Agni deva immediately started bragging about his powers claiming that he would burn the entire earth. To this Yaksha asked Him for a small favor. He put a small blade of grass in front of him and asked him to burn it. Agni Deva was angered by this insult and he tried to burn it but failed to do so. He repeatedly tried to do this act but could not succeed. He felt embarrassed and went back to Indra crestfallen. Indra then sent Vayu Deva who huffed and puffed but could not move that small blade of grass. Varun Deva also suffered the same humiliation and came back without knowing who the Yaksha was. Indra Deva himself decided to go and find out about it and was surprised as the Yaksha had disappeared and, in his place, stood a beautiful Goddess, she was Parvati. Indra inquired about the Yaksha and she revealed His identity as Paramatma himself. She asked Indra to introspect regarding their victory. The victory was a result of Paramatma's grace and not their individual strength. Indra realized his mistake and went back to the Devas and informed them. The essence of the story is the all-doer ship of the supreme being. We easily become conceited and arrogant. Any successful endeavor achieved by us invites pride and ego. We strongly believe that the action was possible because I did it. Wise men believe the other way. More the height achieved by them, the humbler they become. They have a strong conviction in the all-doer ship of the Paramatma. This Profound truth found in the Upanishad requires a high degree of spiritual sadhana under the guidance of a God realized Guru. The fruit of the spiritual sadhana is experiencing the Truth.

Mundaka Upanishad

The Mundaka Upanishad finds its place in the Atharva Veda. It has three main sections called Mundaka and each Mundaka has two subsections called khandas with 64 mantras. It is poetic in style and deals with Brahmavidya. As in the previous Upanishads, we find the style of dialogue between the Guru Angiraas who received this knowledge through a descending line of preceptors beginning with Brahma, the Creator and Sage Shaunaka. Shaunaka asks a very deep and provoking question 'What is that thing, the knowledge of which will at the same time mean knowledge of all things?' To this Angirasa replies, 'There are two kinds of knowledge the lower knowledge (Apara) and higher knowledge (Para). Apara vidya is the worldly knowledge and is considered information. Mere reading or knowledge of Vedas is also included in Apara Vidya. Only that knowledge that frees us from cycles of birth and death and liberates us is Para Vidya. It is knowledge supreme. It is the exponential knowledge of forms, of Atman or Akshara and Paramatma as it is. Once this is known and experienced everything is known. We understood clearly in Chhandogya Upanishad, the dialogue between Sage Narad and Sanatkumar wherein Narad is found to have mastered sixty-four different Vidyas including the four Vedas but was still drowned in an ocean of despair. Sanatkumar conveyed to Narad that all of what he had mastered was just namesake. All of this is included in Apara Vidya or lower knowledge. The Para Vidya or higher knowledge is very complicated, subtle, and deep seated. Mastering Apara Vidya is a requisite for further

Adhyayana of Para Vidya. A certain level of inner purity, intellectual awareness, spiritual inclination, discipline, and a perfect Guru are necessary to begin our journey on the path of Para Vidya.

Mundaka Upanishad explains how Paramatma is independently the cause of all creation in our universe. Just as a spider spins his when required and swallows it back when desired, the same way the supreme being creates the universe and causes its dissolution. He is the matrix and is all pervasive too. He is the sustainer and controller of this universe. We have read about these attributes in the first mantra of Isha Upanishad

ईशा वास्यमिदं सर्वं यत्किञ्च जगत्यां जगत्।
तेन त्यक्तेन भुञ्जीथा मा गृधः कस्यस्विद्धनम् ।।

Isavasyam idam sarvam is a phrase that is used in yogic philosophy to describe the concept that everything in the entire universe is enveloped by God. Idam sarvam means 'all this' - while Isavasyam means 'pervaded by God' in Sanskrit.

In short, Para Vidya is the knowledge of Paramatma. In order to realize the supreme being as it is, we need to surrender at the feet of a God realized guru. Indian tradition places the Guru at the highest position. Previously when kings used to rule our land, their main advisors and counsellors were wise Sages. The kings used to respect them and acted as per their advice. An integrated approach benefitting one and all was always undertaken which resulted in peace and contentment. Here in Mundaka Upanishad, the importance of association with the right guru is the path to self-discovery and realization of supreme cosmic being.

Mandukya Upanishad

This Upanishad rests in the Atharva Veda. It is small with only 12 mantras. The 12 mantras are divided into 4 khandas (sections). Though small it is important as it contains the knowledge of self (atman). It begins with the glory of 'Aum.' Aum is equated here to Brahman. The Soul or Atman is separate from these three bodies (Gross, Subtle and Causal) and three states (Waking, Dreaming and Deep sleep). The main message in this Upanishad is to be aware that the soul transcends the three bodies and three states. Only after understanding the three states in depth, can we understand the fourth stage, which is the Brahmic state. The first is the waking state in which the Atman perceives outer objects with the help of sense organs. We remain aware or are conscious of all our actions and our physical body too. The Atman can experience the outer world of objects.

The second state is the Dream state. During this state the Jivatma cannot perceive outer objects but can perceive inner objects. One is not conscious of the physical body. When we dream, the five sense organs of action and the five sense organs of knowledge are not active. The viewer of the dream is the Atman. The world of dreams is created by Paramatma. In the dream state the Atman experiences the fruits of great many actions (karmas) in a short time. Dream state relates to a Subtle body. The third state is the Deep Sleep state. Here, together with sense organs of knowledge and action, the mind is also inactive. It is a dreamless state. Here, the Causal body is predominant. The fourth state is Brahmic State (Turiya) which transcends all the previous states. It is in this state that self-realization and realization of the supreme being (God) takes place.

Prashna Upanishad

As the name reveals it is an Upanishad in which questions(prashna) are asked by Disciples to their Guru. The Upanishad is found within the Atharva Veda in the Pipalada Shakha.It consists of 67 mantras. The six seekers of Brahmavidya are Bhargava, Kaushalya, Kabandhi, Sautrayani, Sukesha and Satyakama. They came to Pipalada in humility to seek this doctrine of Brahmavidya. The

Guru readily accepts them with love. Guru Pipalada with the intent that a certain level of purification is necessary in order to receive this knowledge, warmly requests them to stay at the Ashrama for a year and practice celibacy and certain Tapas. I feel the space would also provide time needed to develop a warm bond between the Master and students and help in instilling firm faith in the words of the teacher, when they became ready for the sacred Adhyayana. When they fulfilled the Guru's wishes, he called them and said he was ready to answer their questions. The first question was raised by Kabandhi. He asked, "Guruji Who creates this body?" To this the Guru said it is Paramatma. He is the creator and nourisher of all. He is caring and compassionate. He provides all things required to sustain His creation.

The second question was put forth by Bhargava. He asked, "Gurudev how many Devas sustain the body? Among the Devas who is superior?" Pipalada said it is by Paramatma's wish that the 5 elements (Water, Fire, Earth, Air and Space), the five organs of action, the 5 senses and the Prana Vayu work together to sustain the body. Prana Vayu is superior as the body cannot survive without it.

The third question was asked by Kaushalya. He asked, "Gurudev, from where does this Prana Vayu originate? How does it work in the body? To this question Guru Piplada said that Paramatma creates the Prana Vayu. The chief Prana appoints the sub-Pranas; Udana, Vyana, Samana and Apana over different parts of the body.

The fourth question came from Sautrayani. He asked, "Guruji, when a person sleeps which part of the body also rests and which remain active? When asleep who is the creator of dreams and who sustains all? Sage Pipalada says that when one sleeps the sense organs also rest, the hands and feet also rest but the Prana is awake. Whatever we have experienced heard or seen in our life and what we have not comes to us in our dreams. Paramatma is the sole controller of our dreams and the Atman is the witness. Paramatma creates the dreams and then terminates them. In the state of deep sleep there are no dreams. Again, the all-compassionate Paramatma wakes us and by his grace we regain all memory, knowledge, and awareness.

The fifth question came from Satyakama. He asked, "Guruji, when one meditates on AUM what does he attain? Gurudeva replied, "He enjoys oneness with Paramatma and attains Brahmaloka beyond which nothing remains to be achieved. He transcends the cycles of Birth and Death and enjoys eternal peace and joy.

The sixth question was raised by Sukesha. He asked, "Gurudev, I once met a Prince from Kosha, his name was Hiranyanabha and he asked me if I knew a person with sixteen attributes? Guru Piplada says that the sixteen attributes are Prana, Faith, Ether, Water, Light, Air, Space, Senses, Mind, Food, Vigour, Tapas, Mantra, Karma, Loka, and names of the Loka. Only Paramatma is complete in all sixteen aspects. He dwells in our body and so these sixteen facets are also found in Man. In this Upanishad we see a gradual movement from objective experience to the subjective or abstract. The Guru is working on the expansion of consciousness of the disciples. It is only when a certain concept gets absorbed and then gets assimilated deep within, then the next more complicated aspect is revealed by the Master. In short, all Upanishads speak about the supreme consciousness as the ground of reality. This is what creates and sustains the entire universe. This is a very subtle and complex concept not within the capacity of all to comprehend and it requires a Spiritual master's guidance at every step in this Sadhana.

Many of us are under a false notion that this path is meant for those whose intellectual ability is low. Ever wondered why this kind of attitude arose in the first place? For thousands of years devout Hindus practised Sanatana dharma. With the advent of scientific and technological progress, the element of Faith got replaced with Reason and Logic. There is no denial to the fact that both are necessary within limits. With the introduction of Western Education

System, our original Holistic Gurukul system got wiped away. The ancient Gurukul tradition imparted both the worldly knowledge to survive in this physical world and spiritual knowledge for evolution of our consciousness. This system highly improved the scope of producing individuals with high morale. Recent management Gurus also accept this fact. This kind of integrated system of knowledge leads to a high level of refinement in business ethics and this in turn saves our land from loss of crores of rupees which would be funnelled to unworthy people who would use them for their selfish motives. Recent years have been a witness to so many scams. We need to introspect as to what is so seriously wrong. Many of our conscious citizens have pointed out solutions to these problems.

Dr. APJ Abdul Kalam[62] was one great soul. He always dreamed of a developed India. In this context, he coordinated with many intellectuals, experts, scientists, and technologists to plan for a developed India by 2020. The five areas of concern were Education, Health, Agriculture, Information / Communication and last but not the least, Critical Technology. With this on mind, Dr. Kalam visited

---

62 Book Transcendence by Dr Abdul Kalam and Dr Arun Tiwari page 3-4

Pramukh Swamiji in New Delhi. He writes in his book 'Transcendence,' "It was a hot summer evening on 30th June, 2001, when I met Pramukh Swamiji for the first time. Resplendent in saffron robes, the fair complexioned Pramukh Swamiji was radiating divinity. That was the first thought that occurred to me on seeing him."

Then Dr. Kalam presented his Vision 2020 before Swamiji. He explained to Swamiji regarding the five areas taken into consideration for transforming India. Swamiji listened but did not speak. So, Dr. Kalam continued by saying, "Swamiji, our problem is that we may present it to the government but how do we create people with values to realise such an ambitious vision. What we need is a cadre of value-based citizens. For this you are an expert and we need your advice. Pramukh Swamiji smiled and the first words I heard from him was, "Along with your five areas to transform India, add a sixth one that is faith in God and developing people through spirituality. I was taken aback by the clarity and precision and the force of his words. After a pause Swamiji continued, "We need to first generate a moral and spiritual atmosphere. The present system is suffocating and the climate of crime and corruption is toxic to good thought and noble work. This must change. We need to raise people to live by laws of scriptures and God. Without this there will be no transformation." Dr.

Kalam was convinced by Swamiji's response. His scientific mind together with logic and reason was well under balance and control of his spiritual mind. I think there was a perfect alignment of divine energy creating an invisible bridge, a permanent bond of true love which remained between them till his end. He experienced this even when huge distances separated them.

I would call this the quantum connection, wherein communication takes place non locally. Language as a medium of communication is not required. In the above case, the transaction of divine vibrations took place between an ideal Guru and Disciple. For ordinary people this is very difficult as the level required for that to materialise has not been achieved. So, language as a medium is necessary. I think Sanskrit language is an ideal language. All our scriptures are written in Sanskrit which is also the mother of all our regional languages. So, it becomes imperative for Indians to understand the importance of Sanskrit language.

CHAPTER 7

SANSKRIT LANGUAGE AND ITS CONTRIBUTION

Photo by Max Tcvetkov on Unsplash

Antidote

सरस सुबोधा विश्वमनोज्ञा ललिता हृद्या रमणीया ।
अमृतवाणी संस्कृतभाषा नैव क्लिष्टा न च कठिना ।।

Lovely, easy to understand, universally agreeable to the mind elegant, beloved, enjoyable the sweet speech of Sanskrit language is neither obscure nor difficult.

Language is an extremely important aspect of any culture. Especially for Indians Sanskrit is the mother language. For centuries our knowledge, literature, traditions, Spiritual wisdom and way of life have been passed on to future generations in Sanskrit. Our spiritual and cultural foundation lies in this language. We celebrate 5th September as National Teacher's Day in memory of Dr. Radhakrishnan, Independent India's second President. A profound thinker, prolific writer, distinguished scholar, philosopher and most important, a professor. He was a proud Hindu and defender of Hindu Culture. He was offered the post of Professor of Comparative Religion at University of Oxford which he accepted. He was also invited to speak at the University of Harvard. He earned the reputation of being a bridge builder between East and West. This was possible because of his extensive knowledge of western philosophy and literature.

He said, "In case of an Indian youth, he virtually ceases to be an Indian if he does not have an atmosphere of Sanskrit in his temperament either directly or indirectly. It is exceedingly important in order to present the sense of self respect of an Indian educated person that he should have an acquaintance with Sanskrit and its literature. Young men and women passing out of high school and Universities without any knowledge of their National Heritage as preserved in Sanskrit lack the very essential means to approach the outside world confidently with a sense of self-respect. The main reason for this is that this Indian Heritage has got the power to make those who possess it feel a spiritual, intellectual assurance and self-confidence.[63]

Sri Sampurnananda, A teacher, Sanskrit scholar and Political leader said, "There is no language in India which can take place of Sanskrit because no other language has the same intimate contact with the inner spirit of our lives. We may carry the dead weight of English if we choose but it is not and can never be an Indian language. It has no roots in our soil. Sanskrit and Sanskrit alone is associated with the life of the People over the whole country. It is heard in the family circle in the Market place and in the Temple. Let us not play with this great heritage. It can never be replaced but once we lose it, we shall

---

[63] Report of the Sanskrit Commission 1958 - Page 89-90

cease to be Indians. Even our political independence will be of hardly much value either to ourselves or to the world at large.[64]

Gandhiji said, "Sanskrit is like the river Ganga for our languages. I always feel that if it were to dry up, the regional languages would also lose their vitality and power. It seems to me that an elementary knowledge of Sanskrit is essential. It is not sentiment on my part that makes me say so, but practical consideration of the utility to our country of this great language and the vast knowledge held by it.[65]

Swami Vivekananda used to say that the very sound of Sanskrit words gives prestige power and strength to the race. Sanskrit and prestige go together in India. As soon as you have that no one dares to say anything against you.[66]

Dr. Sampadananda Mishra a renowned Sanskrit scholar in his talk has very beautifully described the importance, uniqueness and wonder of Sanskrit language. He says that Sanskrit is not an object specific language. Any word in Sanskrit describes the properties or to use exact word the 'dharma' of that particular object. To cite an example the Amar kosha (Sanskrit) has 32 words for 'water' 'जलम्' is formed

---

64 Sanskrit Vishwa Parishad Bangalore - 1966 (May) Page 42
65 https://www.sanskritimagazine.com/
66 https://vivekavani.com/future-india-swami-vivekananda/

from the root word जल meaning inert (जड). Water has the property to turn from liquid into solid state so the word used is जलम्. Similarly, another word used for water is 'अम्बू' which describes the melodious sound of water droplets. As water flows rhythmically it is called सलिलम्. When we utter or hear Sanskrit words the sounds depict exactly that particular characteristic. Sanskrit language creates an awareness about oneself as well as the environment around us. When language is used with such awareness it brings out the dharma of that object. The whole purpose is to see truth behind the object and not the object itself. Objects are temporary and Sanskrit does not deal with anything temporary. It deals with its dharma which is eternal (शाश्वत). Sanskrit deals with timeless principles and so it is an eternal language. This divine language gives one liberty to form new words. The root sounds are very transparent and so are the prefixes. Sixty to seventy percent of our regional languages are connected with Sanskrit. This is the reason revival of regional languages is crucial for resurrection of Sanskrit.

Sanskrit is a pure and refined language with lots of space for different ideas, the way in which one wishes to express a certain thing or situation. Sanskrit offers ample freedom and this is one of the reasons translations destroys the spirit of this language.

The greatest grammarian in the world to this date is Panini. No one has been able to overshadow him. His work 'Ashtadhyayi' is the best work in Sanskrit Grammar. As the name denotes it has 8 chapters. There are 2000 root sounds mentioned in it. From these root sounds 300 million words are possible. If we check the English oxford Dictionary, it has Twenty-five volumes and Five Hundred Thousand words.

In Sanskrit root sounds are formed from seed sounds meaning individual alphabets. There are more than 33000 root sounds which can form infinite number of words. Each root sound has range of experiences behind it. Each root sound will have fifty meanings, the first being primary and then first level, second level, third level and so on.

According to Dr. Sampadananda Mishra, Sanskrit language cannot be understood intellectually, one must undergo an experiential mode in order to decode meanings. He cites a very good example of how Human Psychology and Natural laws lead to root sounds based on which growth and development of language is interconnected.

He explained the above concept using the word 'संदेह' meaning 'doubt'.

When in doubt there is a psychological phenomenon going on inside the mind. What is the source of doubt? It is not very clear, Sanskrit being a language of awareness self explains the meaning and takes us to the source of the idea.

संदेह is सम् + देह

सम् is a prefix and देह means body coming from root sound दीह् meaning pile, collection, gathering and so on. The physical experience we have with our body is that it grows, it progresses, it enhances, so this is the meaning at second level. As it grows it covers, conceals and hides, so this is the third level. The body is a cover for the soul. This is how we arrive at the meaning. 'संदेह' means perfect covering. When one is in doubt the reality is not seen because it is clouded, meaning our consciousness is clouded. This is how we arrive at the source of 'doubt'. If we look at Vowels and consonants there is a difference. In Sanskrit Vowels are called स्वर and Consonants are व्यंजनानि. Vowels (स्वरः) are अस्पृष्टः meaning sounds without contact because they are free flowing, whereas व्यंजनानि (consonants) are स्पृष्टः meaning 'with contact'. The first alphabet of Devanagari script is 'क'. When we say 'क' that is the first place where obstruction occurs in Oro pharyngeal pathway. At this place the free-flowing sound stops. Dr. Mishra's contemplation on this is very interesting. He says that all words related to questions start with 'क'. When questions arise in mind the free flow of thoughts stop. All interrogative pronouns also start with 'क' e.g., किम्, कुत्र, केन, क्यो, क्या, किससे. To sum up,

He said that Sanskrit language is not framed in our consciousness, it dwells in a different level of consciousness. It is a language of higher consciousness. We can call it a mantric language. The word 'संस्कृत' comes from prefix 'सम्' meaning totality and 'कृत' meaning 'well done' or well sculpted sounds and Vibrations. When these Vibrations are in sync with the universal cosmic, rhythmic meter which holds and sustains the entire creation then its impact is totally different meaning it is powerful, deep rooted and transcendental.[67]

In Mahabhashyam, the great commentary on Panini's 'Ashtadhyayi' Patanjali gives 5 reasons why we should study Sanskrit.

1. रक्षा (Preservation)- For preservation of all our scriptures, yoga, literature, Music, Dance etc.
2. Uha (Modification)- During yagnas the mantras are for one deity but if it is to be used for another deity it must be modified. For this, knowledge of Sanskrit is essential or else the ritual will fail.
3. Agam (scriptural Injunction)- Veda tells us that they should be studied with 6 limbs called Vedanganas, which cover Sanskrit Phonetics,

---

[67] https://www.youtube.com/watch?v=pCuuE6q0p8U | https://www.youtube.com/watch?v=6jRvvwWRx5Q

Phonology, Morphology, Grammar, and Etymology.
4. लघुः (brevity-) shortest way one can study our scriptures.
5. असंदेहः (Unambiguity)- We can unambiguously understand all our cultural heritage, puranas, Vedas, Ramayana, Mahabharata and much more.[68]

Today young people are not clear in seeking right role models. It is very important to associate with wise people who are also spiritually elevated. Today our exposure to outer glamour and selfish motives, devoid of any benefits as seen on larger scale, over shadows the urge to enrich our inner space. We need to rise above all these petty things and seek the right direction and meaning in life.

India has a proud legacy of Educational Institutions and noble personalities who have contributed substantially in different fields. Very few young people want to take interest or delve deeper into this treasure house. One must have the will and intent to journey on this path and I would say beyond doubt, unbelievable rewards wait at the other end. It is essential therefore to know our past which can enrich our present and

---

68 https://www.youtube.com/watch?v=Dw6swQpju7A

ensure a clear-cut future. It hurts deeply to know so many of our Educational Institutions and Libraries have been destroyed and invaluable manuscripts burnt. Western personalities have taken credit for so many discoveries which were already in knowledge of our great Rishis and Teachers. What we studied in school History is not true History at all. Our Historical facts and figures have been distorted or have been excluded from Textbooks.

Dr. Pavan Verma's book "Becoming Indian" is an eye opener for all Indians who are products of post-colonial times. My request to all young Indians is to read this book. He has very clearly explained the effects of Colonization on Indian Psyche and how we should make a conscious effort to reconnect to our roots in order to contribute more positively as Global citizens.

We need to deepen our interest in finding out more about our Grand Narratives. Many Young Indians have already done a lot in this area. Since last many years there has been an active movement for Indic Renaissance. Our original Traditions, Scriptures and Knowledge system were in Sanskrit a language decipherable to few. This was a big disadvantage as the basic knowledge of Sanskrit which was imparted to all students before the British Era was now almost gone. I remember the time I was in Tenth grade in High School back in 1977, we were given a choice for optional subjects. Sanskrit being one of them but majority of the students opted for 'Typing' as the optional subject as it was easier and you could score more. This shows how flawed we are at ground level. Now things are changing for better. Recently some young Indian intellectuals not only from Humanities, but Doctors, Engineers, Lawyers, and scientists armed with sword of logic and reason are now gaining popularity for having dug up the hidden facts and are now spreading awareness regarding it. They have proof and records of everything which they have acquired after meticulous research work. We hear a voice of dissent loud and clear. Our former ignorance is now getting replaced by true knowledge of our glorious past.

The education system of ancient India was not based on materialism only. It was an integrated system aiming at all round development of the individual. Purpose and goal in life was not only acquiring wealth. By this I do not mean that students were not given worldly knowledge but the basis of education was spirituality. Based on this solid foundation, the knowledge of world was given. In those days each village had a temple which imparted primary education to all the children. They were taught about preservation of cultural traditions, customs, environment, basic math, and language. After acquiring basic education those interested in studying further went to larger Temple Universities. India was home to numerous ancient Universities spread all over the subcontinent.

Thousands of temples and educational institutions were destroyed by Islamic invasions. Fifteen ancient Universities of India have been excavated and more archeological work is going on. We will have an over view of a few of these great Universities to have an idea of how progressive and refined our culture and civilization was.

We are all familiar with Takshashila University[69] It is believed that the Kuru prince Duryodhana laid the foundation of this University at the birthplace of his mother Gandhari. This region which is mentioned in Mahabharata as Gandhar is presently in Rawalpindi district of Pakistan. Many ancient Indian Physicians, Politicians, Grammarians, Rulers, Authors, Astronomers studied at this center.

A few stalwarts worth mentioning are the Sanskrit Linguist and Grammarian Panini, famous Physician Charaka, Surgeon Jivaka Komarbacca; Philosopher, Economist, Jurist and Royal advisor Chanakya, Author Vishnu Sharma, King Chandragupta and many more.

---

69 https://www.myindiamyglory.com/2019/02/14/15-ancient-universities-of-india-from-3600-plus-years-ago/

According to the book, 'The Chronology of Ancient India-Victim of Concoctions and Distortions' by Vedveer Arya the Maurya dynasty flourished in 16th century BCE. This means Chandragupta Maurya and Chanakya lived 3600 years ago. This corroborates the antiquity of Takshashila University to be over 3600 years.

Over Sixty courses pertaining to different subjects were taught at Takshashila. It was a center for higher education only. The age eligibility was 16 years, students had liberty to choose subject of his liking. The subjects included Vedas, Vedanta, Vyakarana, Ayurveda Surgery, eighteen Crafts, Warfare, Archery, Astronomy, Agriculture, Commerce, Politics and more. Over 10,500 students from across Aryavarta and from places far as China, Greece, Arabia studied here. It was a residential campus with thousands of teachers.

The second ancient University was Mithila University.[70] This learning center had been in existence since the time of king Janaka, father of Sita. Because of its very ancient timings we do not have archaeological dating to prove it. It was prominent seat of Brahmanical system of Education. Raja Janaka held religious conferences and debates

---

70 https://www.myindiamyglory.com/2019/02/14/15-ancient-universities-of-india-from-3600-plus-years-ago/

where Rishis and Scholars took part. This University taught Literature, Fine arts, Science Subjects, Nyaya and many more. Ganesha Upadhyaya founded a school of New Logic (Navya Nyaya) at this site where he wrote Tatva Chintamani. The Two subjects that later gained prominence in Mithila University were Nyaya (Juris prudence) and Tarka Shastra (Logic). Examination was tough and students received degrees only after they passed (Salakha Pariksha) test after completion of their education.

Third ancient University was located at Telhara,[71] 40 kms from Nalanda University in Bihar. Archaeologists discovered sites in 2014. Chinese travelers Hiuen Tsang and Itsing have mentioned in their Travel accounts about Telhara University as a seat of higher learning and research. It was a competitor to Nalanda University. Bricks used to lay foundation were made of clay dating back to Kushana period which corroborates it to be older than Nalanda University. According to research by Vedveer Arya, Kushana empire flourished between 12th to 8th BCE. This suggests Telhara University to be at least 3000 years old. Hiuen Tsang wrote about a three-storey prayer hall and platform to seat about 1000 monks and students of Mahayana Buddhism.

---

71 https://www.myindiamyglory.com/2019/02/14/15-ancient-universities-of-india-from-3600-plus-years-ago/

During excavations the Archeological Society of India team stumbled upon 1.5-foot-thick layer of ash suggesting it was set on fire by Bakhtiyar Khilji during same time he destroyed Nalanda University in 1193. Khilji was responsible for destruction of three ancient Universities.

The fourth in line is the Sharda Peetha University[72] which flourished as one of the biggest centers of learning in ancient India. At present this institution falls under Azad Kashmir Jurisdiction of Pakistan. Many famous scholars from India and neighboring Countries studied at this famous University. Few scholars worth mentioning are Kalhana, Historian and Author of 'Rajtarangini' History of Kashmir in Sanskrit, Vairotsana a Tibetan translator, Thonmi Sambhota a Tibetan scholar who invented Tibetan script and many more. Sharda Peeth[73] is said to be where texts were written by Panini (Ashtadhyayi). King Jayasimha of Gujarat commissioned Jain scholar Hem Chandra to write Siddha Hema (work on Grammar). Hema Chandra visited Sharda Peeth to access previous works of Grammar. Sharda Peeth once housed Sharda University with over 50 scholars and a huge library. Huan Tsang – Chinese traveler visited Sharda Peeth

---

[72] https://www.myindiamyglory.com/2019/02/14/15-ancient-universities-of-india-from-3600-plus-years-ago/

[73] https://www.dailyexcelsior.com/shardapeeth-the-lost-glory/

in 632 AD and gives an account of his experiences of meetings and discussions with scholars and yogis at Sharda Peeth, who he claims were exceptionally brilliant. Adi Shankara visited Sharda peeth and defeated all scholars over there and won the highest hierarchical position of 'Acharya.'

Swami Ramanujacharya wrote his commentary on the Brahma sutras sitting at the Peeth. It is at this Temple University Adi Shankara received the right to sit on the Sarvajnana Peetham (Throne of wisdom). There is believed to be an ancient tradition among the South Indian Brahmins of prostrating in direction of Sharda Peeth before beginning their Education.

Another very famous University located in the ancient Kingdom of Magadha (present Bihar) is the Nalanda University.[74] Kumar Gupta I is considered as the founder of this great institution. As per Veda veer Arya's book of chronology of ancient India the Gupta era commenced in 335 BCE. This means Nalanda is over 2000 years old. It was principal seat of learning attracting students from as far as Tibet, China, Greece, Persia and beyond until the Turkish invasion of 1193. Nalanda University followed highly formalized methods of Vedic learning besides principles of Buddhism. Admissions to Nalanda

---

74 https://www.myindiamyglory.com/2019/02/14/15-ancient-universities-of-india-from-3600-plus-years-ago/

University was very tough. According to Hiuen Tsang (Chinese traveler) only 20% of students succeeded. 1500 teachers taught here and eight to ten thousand students received higher Education. Education was provided free of cost. There were eight huge buildings in the campus. Subjects taught ranged from Mahayana Buddhism, Vedas, Logic, Sanskrit, Grammar to Medicine, Samkhya and more.

According to Tibetan sources the Library at Nalanda University was spread over three large multistoried buildings. One of the buildings had nine storeys that housed the most sacred manuscripts. Nalanda was destroyed by Bakhtiyar Khilji a Turkish plunderer. He set fire to the libraries and killed teachers (Acharyas) and students. According to an account by Persian Historian Minhaj -al- Siraj in his book Tabaqat-L-Nasiri these manuscripts burnt for several months.

Vallabhi University[75] was set up in line with Nalanda University by the kings of Maitrika dynasty. Maitrikas were feudatories of the Guptas, who established their capital in Vallabhi (Saurashtra, Gujarat) According to Vedveer Arya in his book 'Chronology of Ancient India, this University is at least 2000 years old. Vallabhi University taught

---

75 https://www.myindiamyglory.com/2019/02/14/15-ancient-universities-of-india-from-3600-plus-years-ago/

several subjects including Economics, Law, Politics, Medical Science, Literature, Vyakarana and Hinayana Buddhism. It accommodated a huge library. Quality of education was superlative. It attracted students from all over the country including neighboring countries. Chinese traveler Tsing visited Vallabhi University in 7th century. This Centre was renowned for religious tolerance and mental freedom. The Arabs destroyed it in the 8th century.

Vikramshila University[76] was located 50 kms east of Bhagalpur in Bihar (One North Magadha) and was established by Pala king Dharmapala in later 7th century. Over 100 teachers taught 1000 students. The learning center housed several temples. Around 108 scholars were appointed in charge of the temples. There were six huge colleges with a big building in the center called 'Vigyan Bhavan' All buildings were connected by six gates. Subjects taught were Logic, Philosophy, Vyakarana, Tantra Shastra etc. Bhaktiar Khilji destroyed it in 1205 CE.

Kanthoor Shala[77] was situated in Thiruvananthapuram (Kerala). It taught 64 different branches of knowledge and was called Nalanda

---

[76] https://www.myindiamyglory.com/2019/02/14/15-ancient-universities-of-india-from-3600-plus-years-ago/

[77] https://www.myindiamyglory.com/2019/02/14/15-ancient-universities-of-india-from-3600-plus-years-ago/

of South. It existed between 9th and 12th centuries and was destroyed by Chola attacks. The Charvaka Darshan which was not taught at Nalanda was taught here. Mantra, Yoga, Rasayana (Chemistry), Dentistry, Pediatrics, Fine Arts, Painting, Vocal, Instruments and Dramatics were also taught.

According to Sahana Singh, Author and Commentator based in Texas, US,[78] there was a well-established Ecosystem to support learning. Expenses were subsidized by ruling kings. Nalanda was funded by revenues of 100 villages. Students and teachers received clothes, food, bedding and medicines free of cost. In some ashramas the rich students paid fees while poor Brahmin students did menial Jobs. Financial help was solicited from households too. Ethos of times demanded that Brahmin scholars lead simple lives and engage in pursuit of knowledge without amassing wealth. It fell upon the shoulders of wealthy non-Brahmins and farmers to support those who devoted their entire lives to learning and teaching. Many Sanskrit manuscripts were carried to China either by Chinese scholars or by Indian scholars hired by Chinese kings. Dharma Ruchi a scholar from South India lived in China for

---

[78] https://www.youtube.com/watch?v=vviYeA4fIPM

Antidote

20 years (693 to713 CE) and translated 53 works into Chinese. Dharmakshema was shot by an assassin when two Chinese kings competed for his services. Amogh Vajra collected 500 Buddhist texts from different parts of India and went to China where he translated many into Chinese. Indian Astronomers and Mathematicians from best Universities held high positions in China's scientific Establishments. Indian scientist Gautama Siddha (Qutan Xida) became president of China's official board of Astronomy in 8th century. He translated Navagraha calendar into Chinese. He also introduced Indian numerals to China. Invention of Printing Press is attributed to Buddhist scholars who went from India to China. Printing was used as means to spread Buddhist thought. Indian physician Manka in court of 5th Abbasid caliph translated Sushruta Samhita into Persian. Indian scholars were often invited to Baghdad. The works of Muslim intellectuals such as Al-Kindi, Al-Farabi, Al-Far Ghani, Al-Tabari and Al-Khwarizmi played important role in transferring Indic knowledge of Mathematics, Medicine, Astronomy, Philosophy Chemistry and even music to the Islamic world. While Islamic scholars often credited this knowledge to Indic sources, the European scholars frequently plagiarized from Arabic texts without references. The renaissance was propelled by works of Arabic scholars which were passed off as original works by

Europeans. The Toledo school of translators (12th-13th centuries in Spain got Arabic work translated into Latin.

She further sheds light on Dharam Pal[79] who was an Indian thinker and author. He authored a book 'The Beautiful Tree': Indigenous Indian Education in 18th century. He was instrumental in changing the understanding of pre-colonial Indian education system. He came across archival material of extreme significance in London in 1960s, a series of surveys commissioned by British Government in 19th century to assess the level of indigenous education in India. Every village in India had a Pathshala, there were lakh Pathshalas in Bengal and Bihar alone. Reading, writing, Arithmetic were all taught. The literacy rate was very high. There were dedicated teachers and superior methods of teaching existed with high attendance of students. In large number of schools Shudras outnumbered the Brahmins and Vaishyas.

India was governed for the benefit of Britain. Everything that India produced, food Grains, textiles, steel, gold, silver, minerals was used by British. This led to poverty and hunger. There was no food for teachers and students in Pathshalas. In Thanjavur mass poverty was created overnight by imposing

---

79 https://www.youtube.com/watch?v=vviYeA4fIPM

59% taxation on gross produce. The district collector's role was to fleece citizens. Temples were not spared and had to part with their donations. They fell into despair and are still in that position today. The British Education system sounded the death knell for regional languages.

Mahatma Gandhi said that the British left India more illiterate than it was just hundred years before. Sadly, nothing has changed in our Education system after the British left. Today's education has erased all self-pride from our children and youth. India's self-gaze is still through alien eyes. We know more about Shakespeare but nothing about Kalidasa. We know a lot about Newton, Galileo and Copernicus but are ignorant of Indian stalwarts in different fields of knowledge.

Students are not to be blamed, for since very beginning they have been taught by the same system the British followed when they left. Now that things are changing and that awareness is being seen across the length and breadth of India and among Indians living abroad. It is time to awaken and contribute in any way possible for this very noble cause.

Michael Crichton has rightly said, "If you don't know your history, then you don't know anything. You are a leaf that does not know it is part of a tree."[80]

---

80 https://www.goodreads.com/quotes/188569-if-you-don-t-know-history-then-you-don-t-know-anything

Let us take a brief look at a few of our sages who being spiritually elevated were also stalwarts in field of Medicine, Science, Mathematics, Astronomy, Literature, Poetry and more.

Kashiraj Divodas Dhanvantari[81] was born in 1000 BCE and is considered father of surgery in Ayurveda, the oldest and most holistic field of medical science. His teachings and surgical techniques were compiled by his foremost student Sushruta. He devised twenty sharp and 101 blunt instruments for skilled surgery. Some of the surgical procedures include Lithotomy (removal of stones), Skin Grafting and Rhinoplasty (Repairing mutilated nose). Dhanvantari also made contributions in field of Physiology, Anatomy, Dravya Vignaan that is Pharmacology and Therapeutics. Modern scholars also call him a Molecular Biologist. He gave complete theory of drug composition, molecular structure, physio chemical properties and therapeutic action of foods and drugs. He was first in the world to cite haemopoietic component (blood forming) in liver, role of spleen and liver in forming of blood.

Another very important Medical Expert was Maharishi Sushrut.[82] He conducted a variety of

---

[81] http://www.mysteryofindia.com/2015/04/kashiraj-divodas-dhanvantari-father-of-surgery-in-ayurveda.html

[82] Rishis Heroes and Mystics of India by Sadhu Mukundacharandas – Page 25 to 27

surgeries such as caesarian, artificial limbs, cataract, urinary stones, fractures, and plastic surgery. He noted down everything in Sushruta Samhita. This Book contains 120 chapters in 5 parts with an explanation of 1120 illnesses and details regarding 700 medicinal plants and a detailed study on Anatomy. He was pioneer in use of Anesthesia and promoted use of wine with incense of cannabis for anesthetic purpose. He explained eight types of surgical procedures, excision, incision, scraping, puncturing, probing, sravana apposition and stitching. He described six types of dislocation of joints and twelve varieties of fractures of shaft together with principles of fractures, treatment such as tract manipulation, appositions, and stabilization. He discussed surgical methods of managing hemorrhoids and fistula. His main contribution was towards plastic surgery and cataract surgery.

The next important personality in medical field was Charaka.[83] He is hailed as India's most outstanding ancient medical practitioner. Around 4000 years ago Agnivesha compiled an Ayurvedic treatise called "Agnivesha Samhita" guided by his Guru Rishi Atreya Purnavasu. Around 800 BC Charaka redacted the "Agnivesha Samhita". Charak used to move about the

---

83 Rishis Heroes and Mystics of India by Sadhu Mukundacharandas – Page 33 to 39

country and help people everywhere. The 'Charaka Samhita' consists of 120 chapters under eight categories like diet, food, pharmacology, pathology, prognosis that is outcome of diseases, physiology, anatomy, and embryology. He said that human body is made up of five elements; Earth, Water, Air, Fire and Space. The body's constitution is made up of three doshas or humors, Vatta, Pitta and Kapha. When their equilibrium is disturbed disease sets in. Disturbance in Vatta leads to eighty types of diseases. Forty diseases result due to imbalance in Pitta and Kapha imbalance leads to twenty types of diseases. Two thousand years before Harvey the concept of blood circulation was known in Ayurveda. Charaka described Heart as controlling organ of blood circulation. Charaka even reveals attributes of a person who will not suffer from disease. He says such a person eats healthy diet and is detached from worldly objects; he is the one who thinks deeply before action and is a donor and regards all creatures with equanimity. He always speaks the truth and is ever forgiving and is associated with pious people. Just like Sushruta, Charaka's excellence, and genius as a stalwart among Ayurveda physicians can be attributed to two factors; an enlightened Guru and personal Sadhana. This endowed him with a phenomenal ability to document the medicinal qualities of thousands of plants and minerals during his life time without experimentation.

Coming to the field of Astronomy and Mathematics. Aryabhata[84] was the greatest. He was born in 475 AD. He first gave theories that were rediscovered many centuries later by Scientists of the West. He was the first to gift Algebra to the world. He was designated the post of Kula Pati meaning 'Head' of university. Most Likely he must have been the Kula Pati of Nalanda University. He wrote at least two works 'Aryabhatiya' and 'Aryabhata Siddhant' The latter has not survived but is known through reference in later works. It deals with Mathematics and Astronomy. It is written in 121 stanzas and divided into four parts. It deals with units of time, rotation of earth, revolution of sun, moon and planets, their orbits, diameters, and epicycles. In mathematics section, he describes geometrical figures, their properties, mensuration, simple simultaneous quadratic and linear indeterminate equations, methods for calculating square roots, cube roots and methods of constructing sine tables. He gave us the accurate value of Pi (II) as 3.1416. He was the first astronomer to describe theory of cause of lunar and solar eclipses. The Aryabhatiya placed him at fore front of genius Mathematicians and Astronomers of India. His revelation of earth's

---

84 Rishis Heroes and Mystics of India by Sadhu Mukundacharandas – Page 41 to 45

rotation and orbit around the sun was 1000 years prior to Copernicus's heliocentric theory.

Jyotish (Astrology) is one of the oldest sciences with its roots in Vedas. Excelling all his predecessors in field of astronomy, Varahmihira was aware of gravity a millennium before Newton. He was born in 499 CE near Ujjain. His works include Panchsiddhantika, Vivahpatal, Bruhadjatak, Laghujatak, Yatra and Brihad Samhita. He used a large variety of metrical style in his works. Panchsiddhantika is a text on astronomy with five principles of astronomy. Vivahpatal deals with auspicious times for marriages and yatra for journeys. Bruhadjataka deals with individual horoscopes. It is still regarded as most authoritative work on the subject. Bruhad Samhita is his most celebrated work. It consists of 106 chapters and 4000 shlokas. It includes topics on planets, asterisms, and signs of zodiac. Other topics are Architecture, Geography, Iconography, Ground Water Channels, Characteristics of Swords, manufacturing of Cosmetics and Perfumes, Science of Precious Stones, Botany and more. He regarded shape of earth as spherical. His poetic creativity in Sanskrit has rendered him a jewel of Sanskrit Literature. His uncanny method of locating ground water veins could not have been discovered in a human life time solely by digging. Many of such revelations sprang from his meditative insights just like Rishis of Ayurveda.

Bhaskar Acharya-II[85] was a renowned mathematician. His works Lilavati and Bijganita are considered unparallel, reflecting his profound intelligence. He was born in the year 1114 CE in Vijadavida, Maharashtra. His work Siddhantshiromani is divided into four parts. Lilavati, Bijaganita, Grahan and Goladhyaya. Bhaskar's model and inspirer was Brahmagupta author of 'Brahmasphuta Siddhanta'. He improved upon Brahmagupta's work with thoroughness that eclipsed his Master's. During Bhaskara's time and after, decadence set in. It affected all cultural fields as foreign invasions destroyed and desecrated the land. The Lilavati is so highly acclaimed that it out shines all his other works. One school of Mathematics opines that a person adept in Lilavati can even compute the exact number of leaves on a tree. He wrote the first work with full and systematic use of decimal number system.

This is an extremely brief outline of some of our land's outstanding ancient scientists. One can always gain more knowledge by accessing the literature available in areas wherein these Rishi Scientists have contributed. There is no doubt that Bharat varsha was a Land par excellence.

---

[85] Rishis Heroes and Mystics of India by Sadhu Mukundacharandas – Page 53 to 57

Will Durant (American Author) said, "India was the mother of our race and Sanskrit mother of all of Europe's languages. She was Mother of our Philosophy, Mother through Arabs of much of our mathematics, Mother through Buddha of ideals embedded in Christianity, Mother through village community of Self-government and Democracy. Mother India is in many ways the mother of us all."[86]

The famous Indian Freedom fighter, Philosopher and Author Shri Aurobindo writes about Indian culture in his essay, "A defense of Indian culture." More high reaching, subtle, many sided curious and more profound than Greek, more noble and humane than the Roman, larger, and more spiritual than the old Egyptian, vaster and more original than any other Asiatic civilization, more intellectual than European prior to the 18th century, possessing all that these had and more it was the most powerful self-possessed, stimulating and wide in influence of all past human cultures."[87]

---

86 https://www.azquotes.com/quote/652602
87 https://www.learnreligions.com/sri-aurobindo-top-quotations-1770346

CHAPTER 8

QUANTUM SCIENCE & ANCIENT INDIAN WISDOM

Nowadays it is fashionable for the young generation to introduce themselves as Atheists or Agnostics. But beholding this beautiful, finely tuned universe one cannot help but believe in a Creator.

Einstein[88] one of the greatest scientists of 20th century said, "That deep emotional conviction of the presence of a superior reasoning power which is revealed in the incomprehensible universe forms my Idea of God".

Dr. Abdul Kalam, the missile man of India and the 11th president of India, a brilliant Scientist was blessed with a sharp intellect together with a strong central Spiritual base. He always emphasized on the unity of science and spirituality. A young girl asked him in a letter whether he believed in God to which he wrote quoting Einstein[89], "Everyone who is seriously involved in pursuit of science becomes convinced that a Spirit is manifest in the laws of the Universe, a Spirit vastly superior to that of man."

German Scientist Max Planck[90] (1858-1947) won the 1918 Nobel Prize in Physics for development of the theory of elementary quanta. He is universally recognized as father of modern Physics. He formulated

---

88 https://www.brainyquote.com/quotes/albert_einstein_112016
89 https://www.goodreads.com/quotes/329896-every-one-who-is-seriously-involved-in
90 https://withalliamgod.wordpress.com/

one of the most important physical theories of 20th century, "The Quantum Theory". He contributed to progress of Theory of Relativity and study of Electromagnetic radiation. In his famous lecture 'Religion and Science' (May 1937), Planck wrote, "Both Religion and Science need for their activities the belief in God. God stands for the former in the beginning and for the latter at the end of the whole thinking. For the former God represents the basis for the latter the crown of any reasoning concerning world view.

In concluding his lecture, he said, it is no wonder that the movement of Atheists which declares Religion to be just a deliberate illusion, invented by power seeking Priests and which has for the pious belief in a higher power nothing but words of mockery, eagerly make use of progressive Scientific Knowledge and in a presumed unity with it, expands in an ever faster pace its disintegrating action on all nations of the earth, and on all social levels. I do not need to explain in any more detail that after its victory not only all the most precious treasures of our Culture would vanish but which is even worse also any prospects at a better future.

He said, 'In the whole universe there is no force that is either intelligent or external and so we must therefore assume that behind this force there is a conscious intelligent mind or spirit. This is the origin of matter.

With the advent of Quantum Theory in the beginning of 20th century the foundation of classical Physics was shaken to the core. Newtonian physics covers only a part of reality. It covers only that portion which is perceived by our senses. In classical Physics everything is predictable if you know about parts you know about whole. Anything beyond the level of perception (human) does not exist. It is highly predictable.

The Quantum theory says that electrons are made up of packets of energy called quanta. There is no fixed path the electrons take around the nucleus. They exist as electron clouds in various shells or orbits. Single electron can exist simultaneously at more than one place. Electrons exist in form of possibilities and observation collapses these possibilities in to reality.

Quantum theory says there is no reality without observation, the electron jumps from one level to another energy level without moving through space in between. It just changes its energy state. Quantum Theory sees human beings having conscious and subconscious mind. The subconscious mind is conditioned by different factors and environment. Mostly we act under the influence of subconscious mind. Conscious mind enables us to live in the present. This awareness can result in dramatic changes for a way better life.

Physicists discovered that the Newtonian laws which worked at macro levels did not apply at subatomic levels. Quantum Theory proposed that energy exists as discrete packets known as quanta. Einstein thought something was amiss in Quantum theory, it was incomplete. Niels Bohr challenged Einstein by supporting Quantum theory. He argued that the act of indirect observation of atomic particles changes the outcome of result. Bohr stated that quantum reactions were based on probability. He won the 1922 Nobel Prize in physics for his work on quanta.

In 1900 Max Planck assumed that energy was made of individual units as quanta. He received Nobel Prize in physics in 1918. In 1927 Werner Heisenberg proposed that precise simultaneous measurements of two complimentary values such as position and momentum of subatomic particle is impossible. This came to be known as Uncertainty Principle, to which Einstein's famous comment, "God does not play dice" came into being.

Niels Bohr proposed the Copenhagen interpretation of Quantum Theory which claims that a particle (wave or particle) cannot be assumed to have specific properties or even to exist until it is measured. He said that objective reality does not exist. In short everything exists in form of potential or probabilities.

Einstein believed nothing travels faster than light but Quantum theory stated that subatomic particles communicate instantaneously. Quantum connections are non-local meaning both photons know immediately what other has done. Newtonian physics was deterministic meaning we could determine the evolution of things from established laws that rule matter.

The Upanishads say that the same universe outside is also inside us. So, the underlying reality in ourselves and the outside universe must be the same. Bohr, Heisenberg, and Schrodinger must have had the knowledge of the Vedic texts. Heisenberg[91] stated that Quantum theory will not look ridiculous to people who have read the Vedanta.

Schrodinger[92] wrote in his book Mein Weltansicht, Vedanta teaches that consciousness is singular, all happenings are played out in one universal consciousness and there is no multiplicity of selves. Maya is the cause of our faulty identification with this material world. In all embodied forms of existence Atman is fully able to at any time revive his forgotten eternal and inherent connection with Brahman or

---

91 https://cpdarshi.com/2011/11/22/modern-physics-found-its-direction-from-vedanta/

92 https://www.goodreads.com/en/book/show/1157019.My_View_of_the_World

Paramatma, the supreme self and source of all living entitles.

Schrodinger[93] did not believe that it is possible to demonstrate unity of consciousness by logical arguments. He said that one must make an imaginative leap guided by communion with nature and persuasion of analogies. He understood the non-material eternal nature of conscious self and how Atman is intimately connected to the Supreme.

Einstein also said, when I read the Bhagavad Geeta and reflect on how God created the universe everything else seems so superfluous.

One thing that all this materialistic research has done is open up doors for the world to look deeper into the validity of Vedas for it is stated in our Vedic texts[94] that, 1) A mundane is sure to commit mistakes, 2) is incapably illusioned, 3) has tendency to cheat others, 4) is limited by imperfect senses.

With these four imperfections one cannot deliver perfect information regarding this Transcendental Knowledge. So, no matter how many experiments we conduct we can never come to the absolute truth using imperfect instruments of perception the main being our mind. Intellectual thoughts on platform of

---

93 https://www.krishnapath.org/article/15
94 https://www.krishna.com/forums/4-defects-conditioned-soul

time and space are rendered defective from being subject to four defects shown in our ancient Texts.

Nikola Tesla[95] was a Serbian – American Inventor and Engineer best known for his contributions to the designs of modern alternating current in electricity supply system. He never received the recognition he deserved in spite of being genius in his time. Unfortunately, he was never able to rise to the level of the great Scientists of that time.

Today his accomplishments and creativity are being greatly lauded. He said "Let the future tell the truth and evaluate each on according to his work and accomplishment. The present is theirs the future for which I have realty worked is mine.

Tesla said "All perceptible matter comes from a primary substance or tenuity beyond conception filling all space the Chidakasha or aluminiferous ether which is acted upon the life-giving prana or creative force calling into existence in never ending cycles all things and phenomena.

Diederik Aerts is a Belgian Theoretical Physicist who believes that Reality is not contained within space. Space according to him is a momentaneous crystallization of a theatre for reality where the

---

[95] https://www.goodreads.com/quotes/7468576-all-perceptible-matter-comes-from-a-primary-substance-or-tenuity

motions and interactions of macroscopic entitles (material and energetic) take place. But other entitles like quantum entities for example take place outside space or this would be another way of saying the same thing within a space that is not three-dimensional Euclidean space."

The understanding of universe got revolutionized in late 17th century by work of British Scientist Isaac Newton. He discovered gravity and formulated laws of motion applied to heavenly bodies too. This theory remained valid till Albert Einstein[96] put forward his theory of Special and General Relativity. Einstein stated that speed of light is constant anywhere. Nothing in universe is at absolute rest or absolute motion things just move relative to one another.

$$\text{Speed} = \frac{\text{Distance}}{\text{Time}}$$

When an object moves close to speed of light the time factor slows down. Only then can the speed of light remain constant. This is called time dilatation. So, time is also relative. When an object moves close to speed of light there is length contraction too, so time dilation and length contraction work together to ensure speed of light remains same everywhere.

---

96 https://interestingengineering.com/

Einstein called space and time one entity (space time). Time stops for objects travelling at speed of light and if objects travel at speed more than speed of light time goes backwards and this is not possible so no object can travel at speed of light. Einstein's General theory of Relativity states that objects have mass and they cause warping of space time meaning space time get curved and so objects experience gravitational pull.

Scientists for long debated on whether the universe was steady or ever expanding. By 1990's improvements in ground-based telescopes proved that the universe was expanding at a startling rate. They believed that gravity would gradually slow down the expansion, but research showed that the universe was still expanding at accelerating speeds and this gave rise to theory of Dark matter.[97] Since 1960's astrophysicists have come to accept that there is a whole lot of mass out there which cannot be seen. Theoretically this makes sense but attempts to find dark matter so far has yielded nothing conclusive.

According to Astrophysicists ordinary matter which we can observe is only 5% of total matter. 25% is Dark Matter and 70% is Dark Energy. Dark matter is non baryonic meaning it does not have typical baryonic

---

97 https://www.space.com/20930-dark-matter.html

structure with nucleus electrons protons etc. It may be made up of undiscovered subatomic particles. It does not emit or reflect light. It cannot be picked up by any astronomical equipment. Thousands of clusters of galaxies are moving at a great speed so they should be drifting apart but they are not. Gravitational force is one force which keeps the galaxies from moving apart, but it is not enough there has to be another matter. Scientists calculate mass of large objects in space by studying their motion in center which is moving faster than matter seen on outer edges. They found stars in both locations moving at same velocity indicating galaxies had more mass than could be seen. Clusters of galaxies would fly apart if the only mass they contained were visible to conventional astronomical measurements. Albert Einstein showed that massive objects in the universe bend light allowing them to be used as lenses. By studying how light is distorted by galaxy clusters astronomers have been able to create map of dark matter in the universe. All these methods provide a strong indication that most of the matter in universe is something yet unseen. Although dark matter makes most of the matter in the universe it is only quarter of the total matter. The energy of universe is dominated by dark energy. The universe is rapidly expanding than it was in the past. This would be possible only if universe contained enough energy to overcome gravity and this is dark energy.

Dark Matter does not interact with other matter e.g., light, magnetic force electricity. Dark matter is what makes it possible for Galaxies to exist.

Dark Matter is not antimatter because we do not see unique gamma rays that are produced when antimatter annihilates with matter. Dark Matter is not black holes because black holes are gravity lenses that bend light. Dark Matter composed of black holes would create more lensing events than astronomers detect.

Though modern space technology has been successful in exploring the universe much more than it has in the past, still so much remains a mystery. We see only the tip of the iceberg. I do not think looking at the enormity and vastness of the universe that a breakthrough will be possible using only scientific methods.

We again come back to the fact that our sensory perceptions and intellect are limited. So, the whole truth is always obscured. When someone claims that our Rishis or Seers could see the whole truth it is ridiculed and sent into a box labeled superstitions. Conventional thinking will get us nowhere near the truth.

Dr. Radhakrishnan[98] writes in his book, 'The Principal Upanishads,' "The truths are said to be

---

[98] Principal Upanishads by Dr. Radhakrishnan – Introduction, Page 22

breathed out by God or visioned by Seers (Sages). They are utterances of the Sages who speak out of fullness of their illumined experience. They are not reached by ordinary perception inference or reflection, but seen by the Seers even as we see not infer the wealth and riot of color in summer sky. The Seers have the same sense of assurance and possession of their Spiritual vision as we have of our physical perception. The Sages are men of direct vision. They say that the Knowledge is not discovered by them but revealed to them without their effort. Though Knowledge is an experience of an independent Reality which impinges on his Consciousness. There is an impact of the real on spirit of experiences.

Scientific understanding assumes that an object can be known if it is broken down into its simpler constituents. Anything organic cannot be handled this way. Mechanical unity comes into being by assembling the unit parts together, but organic unity is just the opposite e.g., a seed sown in soil grows from within to the outside and finally to its end stage. This means that the whole cannot be equal to sum of its parts. It also means that when one part is affected the whole experiences the effect. Similarly, an effect in one part of universe will spread all around the universe. So, what is the conclusion? Our universe is alive!!! One of the greatest proponents of this theory is

Dr. Amit Goswami,[99] a theoretical physicist, mentions in his book, 'The self-aware universe.' Once we accept quantum non-Locality as an established physical aspect of the world in which we live, it becomes easier within science to conceive of a transcendent domain outside of the physical domain of space and time. He says that the old school of scientists believed in upward causation, meaning elementary particles came together to form atoms and molecules and then cells which come together to form brain and then consciousness so consciousness is a brain product. But quantum science is a science of probabilities which actualize on observation. So, it proves that by following Quantum theory you get possible consciousness. Upwards causation does not apply here. It is downward causation; consciousness is the ground of all being. Consciousness is non material and it is consciousness that actualizes all matter.

Pope Benedict XVI (Joseph Ratzinger)[100] said, "No scientist could even begin to work unless and until he assumed that the aspect of nature, he was investigating was knowable, intelligible and marked by form. But this fundamentally mystical assumption rests upon the conviction that whatever he comes to know through his scientific work is simply an act of

---

99 The Self-Aware Universe by Dr. Amit Goswami
100 Transcendence By Dr. Abdul Kalam – Page 30

rethinking or recognizing what a far greater mind has already conceived".

The central lesson of the Upanishads centers on the notion that all beings in this world are sustained by the energy of the Supreme Cosmic Self, in other words (Paramatma). It is the ground of all Reality.

We have seen in the Upanishads the importance of Great Gurus. The dialogues between the illumined Gurus and their brilliant students form the framework of Upanishads where in metaphysical questions raised by disciples are answered by the Guru.

We have also seen that the Great Teachers initiated disciples only after a certain level of refinement and purity was found in speech thought and action. The masters instructed disciples step by step after knowing the level of comprehension and receptivity present in each student. The teachers themselves were men of very high stature pure in thought and action. It is this purity of character which made possible the transmission of knowledge which in turn elevated their thought processes so as to lead them further up in their quest for Spiritual knowledge.

This is the story of the Upanishad Era and we might ponder regarding its relevance today. Every day the news media is loaded with scams and scandals in every area including religion. We hear about fake Fakirs, Gurus and God men whose sense of morality and righteousness have fallen way below sensibility. It is only natural that people today are not ready to believe in it. The point to introspect is, how can we form an opinion based on something we see or hear a few times? It does not grant us the liberty to generalize and label it negative. If we imagine our culture as a huge tree and the Vedas and Upanishads as its roots and the Sanatan Dharma as the trunk and diverse beliefs as the branches and leaves, if few leaves do rot, we should not worry much as they would eventually fall off but if the roots are firm and healthy there is no danger. Connecting to the roots is important as it will strengthen our faith and raise our self-esteem and create pride in our mind and heart in belonging to this great civilization.

CHAPTER 9

A SPIRITUAL MASTER UNPRECEDENTED

Photo by Karsten Winegeart on Unsplash

Antidote

The bygone era was witness to great civilizations around the world. The Egyptian, Sumerian, Babylonian, Mayan, Aztec, and Indus to name some of the most important ones. Except the Indian civilization all others have disappeared. What is it in ours, that has kept it alive, despite adverse circumstances to which it has been constantly exposed. For centuries India has been invaded and its treasures marauded. But India or more apt 'Bharata' has never invaded other countries. Why so?

Dr. Abdul Kalam[101] during one of his meetings with Pramukh Swami asked the reason why India had never invaded other countries? Swamiji said, "It is a virtue of God". It is the Ishavasya sentiment never to seize something that does not belong to us. Burning global issues cannot end by conferences and summits, but need spiritually elevated souls who are capable of instilling values, morals, and Spirituality in others. War and violence are born in minds of men, then comes the external projection. Dr. Kalam[102] in his book 'Transcendence' puts forth a beautiful thought, He says, "It is my belief that a person's conscience develops at a pace at which his relationship with God develops and as both develop the inner voice which is available to us becomes

---

101 Transcendence By Dr. Abdul Kalam – Page 05
102 Transcendence By Dr. Abdul Kalam Page 65

stronger and more reliable as a guide for the action one plans."

Dr. Kalam had immense love for Pramukh Swamiji. Several teachers had contributed quite a lot in his life but for him Swamiji became his ultimate teacher. Despite language barrier both used to communicate in a profound Spiritual way. Swamiji loved Kalam for his purity of mind and action. He used to call him a Rishi. It would sound surprising as to how two so different individuals could manage to come so close. This is the proof that spiritually aware persons are Transcendent. They are way above the barriers of caste religion and gender. They communicate at soul level. They are in constant communion with the Supreme Cosmic Self.

A glance into the life of Pramukh Swamiji would leave us bewildered as it is beyond our comprehension when we look at the magnitude of his achievements in a single lifespan.

Swamiji was born on 7th December 1921 as Shantilal to a farmer family in Chansad a small village a few kilometers away from Vadodara (Gujarat). His name revealed his nature for he was an epitome of peace. Anyone who came near him also experienced the same tranquility. He rose to become the spiritual and administrative head of BAPS (Bochasanwasi Akshar Purushottam Sanstha). Born to pious and devoted parents and his childhood was normal as others of his time except for his natural spiritual inclination which was visible to all around him. He often used to think and dream about the Himalayas and places like Haridwar with a deep longing to be there. He was extremely quiet, and soft spoken when the need arose to speak, which he rarely did. He never demanded anything, a quality which made his mother take extra care of him. At the young age of 18 he was initiated into monkhood (Sadhu) by his Guru Shastriji Maharaj. Shastriji Maharaj foresaw the tremendous spiritual potential in Pramukhswamiji and showered his blessings and grace on him whenever the chance arose. Life during those times was not easy and he had to face many adversities but with his strong conviction in God and his Guru he was able to overcome one and all. Obstacles were stepping stones for him; he never feared them. He was able to achieve unimaginable feats with his perseverance and hard work. What Albert Einstein wrote about Gandhi, that generations to come will scarce believe that such a one as this ever in flesh and blood walked upon this earth, remained true for Swamiji.

As we read his biography, and look at his initial years in presence of both his Gurus and then later as the Spiritual and Administrative head of BAPS, our mind refuses to grasp the immensity of his contributions for the betterment of our society.

A very warm and loving heart, eyes so transparent and pure, his hands always eager to help. His feet toiled without rest in order to ease people's sorrows. Swamiji was an embodiment of selfless love and humility. Spiritually so elevated yet so much approachable to ordinary mortals that one lost track of the vast difference in substance. There could never be any comparison for he was transcendent, way above our mundane world, yet he stooped down low to our level to comfort us and lift us out of misery. He was a master visionary and under his able leadership BAPS organization flourished immensely. In this matter he never compromised on the ideals and principles laid down by Bhagwan Swaminarayan and his Gurus. His clarity of thought was never smudgeable but solid and firm. Wherever he stepped differences dissolved, animosity melted, borders disappeared, people one and all came together to experience his divine love and touch. A rare jewel among priceless virtues that adorned Pramukh Swami Maharaj was his humility. It stood out pure and clear amidst his magnanimous personality. Despite his highly elevated spiritual stature, he could instantly connect with people from varied strata of society, including children, youth and old. Generation gap never existed for him. Deception never hovered around him. His transparency and honesty reached uncharted heights. People experienced unprecedented joy and peace in his divine presence and permanent bridges were built across hearts. Swamiji's silent love broke barriers of language and communicated deep down to soul level. When he spoke lofty ideals and great Spiritual truths got transformed into simple comprehensible easy to digest practical solutions for Spiritual aspirants.

Someone has rightly said, "Eyes are the window to the soul". A single glance at his eyes one could witness compassion, peace, and tranquility together. His heart and soul held God, God alone. There was never any place for baser passions and petty trivial acts within him. Swamiji looked human to us when we beheld him with our outer eyes but a single honest attempt to delve deeper would reveal divinity in its highest form. This too was possible only with his Grace. He showered his Grace unconditionally to one and all. Borders of caste, creed and land disappeared in his divine vision. He visualized each being at the core of his existence, the essence of being that is the soul (Atman). The Atman carries no burden of worldly garbage, for it is Sat- Chit- Ananda. To enjoy this divine bliss is the birth right of every human being. Realization of this state makes one eligible to move ahead on the path of being one with the supreme cosmic self (Paramatma).

Swamiji's most powerful strength lay in his unwavering singular faith in God. His strong conviction in the all-doer ship of God led him across all hurdles in life, and was a source of inspiration for all his followers. This spirit of deep faith in God made his life God – centric and from here arose power to achieve everything he sought for the betterment and transformation of human kind. Doctors attending him were mesmerized and touched by his divinity. Atheists turned into believers. People with prejudices, biases and wrong opinions were at once transformed on meeting him. This was the experience of not one or two but thousands who came to him. He had a beautiful mind, a mind filled with pure and noble thoughts. This had a tremendous positive effect on people he interacted with. They got healed and changed forever. Such was Swamiji's transformative power. It was this quality in Swamiji which initiated and established a deep sense of security in all who sought refuge at his feet.

Dr. Kalam says in his book 'Squaring the circle' "All scriptures say that human potential is fully realized when we contribute to the planet at spiritual level. When we function at material level our potential is underused and even misused." The centers of spiritual energy are Mandirs (Temples) in our culture. He was a Master Temple builder. He firmly believed that Mandirs were centers for spiritual and moral progress. Mandirs are hallmarks of cultural identity. It is through Mandirs that traditions are passed on through generations. They give us a strong sense of belonging. Mandirs have no borders and they symbolize "unity in diversity". The term Unity in diversity is Pluralistic. Pluralism in the sense that there are many ways leading to the same ultimate truth. One is free to choose his or her path.

Dr. Kalam[103] had once asked Pramukh Swamiji, "why build Temples? What purpose do they serve"? Swamiji said, "Mandirs are the physical manifestation of the Unseen." When we hear about self-realization or soul realization it seems abstract to us for it is beyond our sense perceptions. We need something concrete to concentrate or stabilize our restless mind. Mandirs help us in this process. The Mandirs are filled with positive and divine vibrations because of sacred rituals, mantras, and prayers. The atmosphere is pregnant with divinity and so it becomes a lot easier for a spiritual aspirant to progress in one's sadhana.

The soul of the mandir are the Murtis. They have been consecrated by extensive idol installation rituals. Sacred mantras are recited from Vedas. The supreme self is all pervading and manifests through the murtis. Mandir is a place of utmost faith for believers. Mandir is a connector to the vast cosmos the living universe and finally the Supreme Reality. Mandir space is such that the mind naturally withdraws inwards becomes calm and effortlessly meditates or worships. Such a

---

103 Transcendence By Dr. Abdul Kalam – Page 57

mind becomes field for moral upliftment. Values tend to take a firm hold and baser passions like anger, envy, greed, deceit, and ego diminish and disappear. Peace and joy become our natural partners and from within arises the courage to override adverse circumstances with absolute calmness.

Swamiji's life was a testament to innate good, simplicity and truth. His magnetic personality attracted youth with fervor unmatched. So many youngsters gave up comfortable lives and luxuries to be with Swamiji. Some of them renounced homes to be initiated into monkhood, a decision in no way easy considering the hardships, mental and physical which show up on this path. Swamiji's love was never on the material plane, it was transcendent and this resulted in transformation of youths to lead their lives for a mission far larger and superior than they would have had in worldly affairs. Renunciation demanded rigorous discipline both physical and mental. With Swamiji's love and nurturing these sadhus walk the path less travelled and serve the society in many different and useful ways. Today I would call it a ripple effect created which is expanding and all embracing.

In his book 'Transcendence' Dr. Kalam[104] says, "There is a lie that acts like a virus within the mind

---

104 Transcendence by Dr Abdul Kalam page 189

of humanity. And that lie is that there is not enough good to go around. There is scarcity and there is limitation and there is just not enough. The truth is there is more than enough good to go around. There are more than enough creative ideas. There is more than enough power. There is more than enough love. There is more than enough joy. All of this begins to come through a mind that is aware of its infinite nature. There is enough for everyone. If you believe it, if you can see it, if you act from it, it will show up for you. That is the truth, that is what truth seekers must understand."

Swamiji strongly believed that all human beings are innately virtuous. If children are not nurtured in a positive environment, they gradually lose these virtues. Focusing on academics only is the greatest mistake parents make. The external environment and pressure are high and so is the competition. In this fast-globalizing world we are losing our identity and are fast accepting and following western ideas. Our priceless Scriptures are gathering dust because interest in studying them is almost nil. We are unaware about our Grand Narratives. There is no sense of belonging or pride. Morality, ethics, and values are ebbing. To move against the current trend and to try and re-establish our lost glory is no trivial thing. Swamiji worked tirelessly till the age of 94 for this. He met more than 20 million people in his life time. He read and wrote 7.5 lacs letters, visited 60 countries, 17000 villages. He was the administrative head of BAPS for 65 years and spiritual head for 45 years. The above figures seem impossible in a life time but are true. Swamiji's time management skills were matchless. He never wasted even a second. He would perform two to three activities at one time. He was never late for any appointment. For many years his waking time in the morning remained same but sleeping time was erratic. These figures reflect the magnitude of his selfless service towards betterment of lives. How could he answer so many letters? Well, he answered for sure. What did people write to him? Well, they asked for solutions and blessings for the day-to-day problems and woes they faced. Very few requested his guidance regarding Spiritual Sadhana. That did not matter to him at all for he answered each letter with love, care and consideration. It is not an exaggeration to mention that he had touched the lives of all his followers and many others too.

Once during a Satsang assembly, one of the saints addressing the Sabha raised a question as to how many had personally met Pramukh Swamiji and hands went up. Next, he asked how many had connected with Swamiji through telephone and many more hands were raised. Lastly, he asked, 'How many communicated to him through letters and all the remaining hands went up. Not a single devotee was left. Such was his dedication and selfless love. He believed it was his bhakti towards his Gurus and God.

The number of villages he visited included the tribal areas of Gujarat where literacy was at an ebb and alcohol, drugs and tobacco abuse had resulted in inhuman conditions for women and children. People believed in Black magic, superstitions, and other harmful traditional practices. It was no easy task to reform these people. But Swamiji, his saints and volunteers have worked tirelessly for years. This work was appreciated by the government officials too. Under his inspiration De addiction camps and literacy campaigns also materialized and were successful. Whenever Natural Calamities created havoc and the need arose for assistance, be it food, clothes, medical aid; Swamiji was one of the first to respond. Even during the covid pandemic BAPS organization's contribution was noteworthy. During the drought years (1987-88), Swamiji motivated his saints and followers to set up cattle camps and requested farmers in Gujarat to grow grass for these cattle. For the ordinary farmers oxen are their life line and during drought time it was impossible for farmers to take care of their cattle. In such trying times Swamiji immediately took decisions and saw to the implementation of the project regarding the cattle camps. Other festivals and celebrations were cancelled and complete priority was given to this project. Swamiji's cattle camps were extraordinary in terms of care and consideration. He personally visited the sites and gave instructions wherever necessary. Animals were also given medical care. The owners were allowed to stay with their oxen and were looked after in all ways. When time arrived for the oxen to leave, they were all strong and in excellent health, ready to plough the fields. The owners also left transformed like never before, as they got rid of many vices and addictions. Swamiji made life so pleasant for them. In short it was a LIFE DIVINE….

His life was lived for others in the sense that others' lives were better lived and long-lasting peace and harmony prevailed. His life was an open book full of inspiring, lofty ideals and spiritual truths combined with simplicity and treasure house of tips for loving productive life both worldly and spiritual. Whosoever met him once would never be able to forget the divine experience. His Holiness Swami Chidananda Sarasvati (Divine Life Society – Rishikesh) had great love and affection for Swamiji. He said, "Pramukh swami is Narayan incarnate he is jewel among sages." His lustrous persona and exemplary moral life spread a divine aura. It lights the way for all people to lead morally pure and God centered lives. I can see the aura of saintliness, brotherhood and world harmony radiating around him. Bhagwan Ram is known as Maryada Purushottam. Pramukh Swamiji is today's Maryada Purush (sadhu of morality).

Our scriptures say:

दुलर्भं त्रयमेवैतत् देवानुग्रहहेतुकम ।
मनुष्यत्वं मुमुक्षत्वं महापुरुषसंश्रयः ।।

These three are rarely obtainable in this world and depend on Grace of God; the Human birth, Desire for salvation and company of Great Souled ones.

Swamiji could never belong to few, he belonged to the world in entirety. He belonged to all those who connected with him in different ways and were blessed to be inspired by his lofty ideals, way of life, his practical solutions to life's miseries and lastly the path to Self-realization and eternal liberation from endless cycles of birth and death. (Moksha).

Dr. Kalam[105] mentions in his book, 'Transcendence, "When I sit with Pramukh Swamiji, I feel through his eyes the universe perceives itself and through his ears is listening to its harmonies. Pramukh Swamiji is a witness through which the universe becomes conscious of its glory and magnificence. When I sit with him, I feel everything is connected. Non-Violence

---

[105] Transcendence By Dr. Abdul Kalam – Page 196

is an expression of this interconnection. Leaves of the tree affect direction of the wind and way the pollen drifts. The way light reflects in Pramukh Swamiji's eyes illuminates reality."

His biography is midway at the present time. This extensive work by Pujya Adarshjivan Swami reflects about his extraordinary life but collectively so many feel that it is just the tip of an iceberg. Swamiji's life was unparallel, supremely benevolent together with meaning and substance. This is the reason it is not possible to confidently say, 'This is it' for so many lives have been touched blessed and inspired by him and have not been in records. Even after he passed away hundreds and thousands thronged in long queues to have his last darshan. This was the kind of influence he exerted on the masses which included his devotees.

Today as I write these words saints and volunteers are working tirelessly to keep his heritage alive and moving forwards. This is possible only because Pramukh Swamiji's divine legacy is being carried forward by His Divine Holiness Mahant Swamiji (Keshavjivandas) under whose inspiration and love the world experiences the same sacred vibrations and actions unfolding. We remain indebted to him forever. Coincidently this year is Swamiji's Birth Centenary year and Ahmedabad has been fortunate to organize this Grand Festival taking place between

December 15th and January 15th 2023. It is going to be one of the most memorable events in history. We can consider ourselves very lucky to witness this grand event where we will be able to witness the life and work of Swamiji and the ideals, values and vision of a beautiful world he envisaged.

CHAPTER 10

MANDIRS: CONNECTORS TO THE COSMOS

Mandirs have long been the sacred places dedicated to Worship, Rituals, and Prayer. Mandirs are not only visually attractive but display an invisible aura of Divinity which can be experienced by the devotee. I feel Mandirs are connectors to the Cosmos. If we think about the differences in Architecture when observing a Mandir and viewing a House or a building which is aesthetically pleasing there is a vast contrast. A beautiful House or a Building will create a sense of joy in our minds which will ebb away with time while emotions on sight of a Mandir will generate bliss which is totally on another plane. The thoughts we have when entering a Mandir or another Building are also very different. Thoughts when looked at conceptually are Energy Vibrations. A Mandir will generate vibrations which are out of time and space and so remain with us eternally while a beautiful building or a house will form vibrations within the confines of Space and Time. These vibrations are short lived just as it is for all material objects. Mandirs take a form so that it is easy for the devotee to perceive that which is out of reach of senses. For all this to make sense one must come in Faith else everything is futile. The element of Faith is the foundation on which rests the whole Divine Experience. The sound of the Shankha and Bells falling on the ears immediately connects us to the Divine vibrations symbolizing an Entity transcending this realm. It has a soothing and calming effect on the mind. The distracted and clouded mind gathers itself and becomes ready for the Divine Darshan of the presiding Deity. Whatever change is experienced by the mind is also supported by the heart for it is the seat of pure love. One feels absolutely relaxed and in the state of meditation while awake. The magnificent domes symbolize the vastness of the universe where sounds resonate with supernatural vibrations. The receptivity of the brain increases and the body and mind are in perfect order to align exactly as required for the Darshan. Sounding of the drums create within us a longing for the Darshan of the Deities who are still out of our view. As the majestic Doors open and our eyes behold the pious Forms an extraordinary emotion rises within the heart and we experience Goosebumps and feelings of utter Bliss as the lotus eyed Divine murtis bless us with utmost compassion and immense power, the power to wipe out our baser passions. The light of the 'Aarti' reflects radiance abound and one feels devoid of any worldly sorrows pain and plight. This is the unlimited power we experience of our real Self. I feel this experience is common for all devotees who come to worship in faith. This is the way God communicates with us silently but omnipotently. Purer the heart, cleaner the mind the more we can connect with him.

Antidote

Mandir is a place of collective worship. So many devotees enter the pious place with faith in heart and a mind devoid of ills. The sacred vibrations of this collective worship emanate and pervade everywhere in the mandir and this results in healing of soul and mind. Atmosphere is filled with divinity. Mandirs are usually towering, massive with huge sculpted entrances and majestic doorways which leave us in awe. As soon as we enter the Mandir premises all our worldly or materialistic loads disappear and we get transported to another realm abound in pure love and tranquility. There is a kind of magnetic pull we experience; communication is not always in words. At the mandir one does not require medium of language in order to communicate. The sound vibrations are enough to do so and if the sound is missing the silence does the work equally well. Silence in the Mandir is also different, it is a soothing silence, one that makes you want to introspect. Inherent nature of man is to remain in 'Ananda' [blissful joy]. The worldly burdens weary us and we become more body centric forgetting the real Self. The Mandir environment is conducive to Spiritual elevation. One can work towards expansion of consciousness which is the goal of human life. Mandir plays a very important role in this human endeavor.

One of the most magnificent temple architectures which captures my mind and heart is the majestic

Akshardham temple situated on the banks of river Yamuna in our capital city New Delhi. Akshardham was the vision of Yogiji Maharaj, Pramukh Swamiji's guru. It was created under the inspiration of Pramukh Swamiji with the purest of intentions and reflecting and serving as a symbol for all that Bharata, this glorious Nation represents in areas of Art, Culture, History, Heritage, and Spirituality.

The traditional temple builders of India also known as Sompuras gave estimated time to create a temple of this grandeur to forty years. The story of its making is an unbelievable aspect because this splendid monument was created in a record time of five years. How this was possible is another astounding tale. This astronomical Mandir is built of stone and no steel has been used at all. It contains 234 ornately covered pillars, 9 carved domes, 20 samvarans (pyramidal roofs), and a plinth of stone elephants (Gajendra peeth). Two thousand murtis and statues of India's great sadhus, devotees, acharyas and divine personalities adorn the Mandir. The Mandir is 141 feet high, 316 feet wide and 356 feet long. It is a fusion of pink stone and pure white marble. In the center of the mandir is the 11 feet high golden murti of Bhagwan Swaminarayan and Guru Parampara(hierarchical)Murtis too. One of the main attractions of the temple is "Neelkanth yatra" a large format film which depicts the 12000 km long pilgrimage undertaken barefooted by 11-year-old Neelkanth Varni (Bhagwan Swaminarayan) across the length and breadth of India spanning 7 years. All those involved in the project whether construction or the film shooting and other aspects unanimously agree that the project could not have been completed without divine intervention. Thousands have visited the complex and have returned back with divine memories and transformation. Many lives have been enriched and have taken a turn for the better and this continues even today.

His Holiness Jeer Swamiji (Ramanujacharya Totadri Tamandu) has truly said, Akshardham will be the greatest inspirational place in the world for revival of Hindu dharma. It is simply wonderful. I would not be exaggerating in saying that there is no architecture comparable to this. I have seen with my eyes many beautiful and wonderful buildings but Akshardham is unparallel and incomparable.

Mandirs have always been a very important aspect of our culture since time immemorial. In ancient India all the villages had mandirs which were important centers for worship, spirituality and education. Ours has been one of the greatest civilizations in the world. If we consider reasons for the highly enduring and still prevalent cultural traditions and heritage which have lasted amidst barbaric invasions and foreign rules. I must say the Mandirs have played a very influential role. Mandirs since ages have sustained and nurtured the spirit of man. They preserved our ancient rituals, manuscripts, traditions, ceremonies, way of worship, knowledge and much more. So many other great civilizations of the world today lie in ruins while ours, though it has endured centuries of destruction and violence, stands firmly rooted to the soil. No amount of force, threats or violence has been able to diminish the bright burning light of this great Nation.

The soul of this country are its Scriptures, the splendid magnificent Mandirs and its Sages and Saints. This is what has kept the spirit of this Country alive. This was the foundation on which the whole of Bharatvarsha flourished and prospered. In ancient India people were spiritually elevated, morally pure and refined. Naturally the country prospered economically and had a GDP of 25% of the world at one time. We suffered because we were hit at the foundation level. We were robbed of our languages, traditions, customs, I would say total way of life. Our original systems were broken down. We were declared independent in 1947. We rejoiced and celebrated not quite aware of the invisible prison we chose to remain in. Our original way of thinking, creativity, reasoning and functioning was lost. We ended up following an alien way of life. It is like a lock we are trying to open with wrong key. It's never going to open up. Our original way of life, thinking, the way we conduct at different levels in the society in the past was the right way. We must go back and reconnect to our glorious Culture and pay attention to all that we have neglected for ages, our Languages, Art forms, Music, Education, History, Spirituality, and the list would go on and on.

We can retain our Cultural identity, also remain faithful to all that is ours and still be global citizens. I would like to conclude with a very soul stirring quote by Dr. Radhakrishnan. He says, "It is the intense spirituality of India and not any great political structure or social organization that it has developed that has enabled it to resist the ravages of time and the accidents of history."[106]

This is the way walked by our Rishis, Saints, Philosophers, Poets, and Ordinary people too.............. Do give it a try ....!!!

---

[106] https://www.goodreads.com/quotes/1189023-it-is-the-intense-spirituality-of-india-and-not-any

CHAPTER 11

THE WONDER THAT IS AYURVEDA

Photo by Conscious Design on Unsplash

Antidote

समदोषः समाग्निश्च समधातु मलःक्रियाः।
प्रसनात्मेन्द्रियमनः स्वस्थइतिअभिधीयते।।
(सुश्रुत संहिता सूत्रस्थान 15/10)

An individual who maintains a balanced state of the main elements of the body including Dosh and Dhatu, adequate digestion (Agnee), proper excretion (Malkriya), blissful condition of soul (Atma) satisfied senses (Indriya) and happy state of mind (Manas) is called Swastha Person

Dr. Rupert Sheldrake[107] is a very well-known Biologist from Cambridge. His theory of morphic resonance is very famous. He has authored more than 90 scientific papers, nine books and co-authored six books published in 28 languages. He was among the top 100 Global thought leaders for 2013 as ranked by Detweiler Institute, Zurich. Switzerland's leading think tank.

According to Dr. Sheldrake there are ten dogmas in science.

1. Universe is mechanical (Machine)
2. Matter is unconscious
3. Laws of constants remain same.

---

[107] https://www.academia.edu/39683324/Sheldrakes_10_dogmas_of_science

4. Energy / matter are constant.
5. No Goal or purpose of life.
6. Biological inheritance is mechanical [has been disproved since discovery of Genome].
7. Memory is stored in brain in form of chemicals (chemical trace)
8. Mind is inside your brain
9. Psychic phenomena are illusory.
10. Mechanistic medicine is the only one that works.

Dr. Bruce Lipton[108] a very well-known Molecular Biologist writes in his book 'The Biology of Belief.'

"Once I finally grappled with quantum physics, I realized that when we so cavalierly dismissed those energy-based practices we were acting as myopically as the chairman of the Physics department at Harvard University who as described in 'The Dancing Wu Li Masters' by Gary Zukav warned students in 1893 that there was no need for new PhD in physics (Zukav 1979). He boasted that science had established that the universe is a matter machine made up of physical individual atoms that fully obey Newtonian mechanics. For physicists the only work left was to refine its measurements.

---

108 The Biology of Belief by Dr. Bruce Lipton, Page 69-71

Three short years later the notion that the atom was the smallest particle in the universe fell by the wayside with discovery that atom itself is made up even smaller subatomic particles. Even more earth Shattering than the discovery of those subatomic particles was the revelation that atoms emit various strange energies such as X-rays and radioactivity. At the turn of 20th century, a new breed of physicists evolved whose mission was to probe relationship between energy and structure of matter.

Within another ten years physicists abandoned their belief in a Newtonian material Universe because they had come to realize that the Universe is not made up of matter suspended in empty space but energy.

Einstein[109] revealed that we do not live in a universe with discrete, physical objects separated by dead space. The universe is one indivisible dynamic whole in which energy and matter are so deeply entangled it is impossible to consider them as independent Clements.

According to Dr. Bruce Lipton the body is not a physical machine operating on basis of Newtonian Physics. The body cannot be studied relying on reductionist method. The reductionist method

---

109 Biology of Belief by Dr. Bruce Lipton, Page 72-77

or model suggests that if there is a problem in the system, source of problem can be attributed to malfunction in one of the steps along the chemical assembly. A Drug is given which repairs that single point and health is restored. However, quantum perspective reveals the universe to be an integration of interdependent energy fields that are entangled in a meshwork of interactions. There is massive communication among physical parts and energy fields that make up whole.

The flow of energy according to Newtonian principles is linear whereas in quantum-based paths its holistic. Dr. Lipton in his research on blood vessel cells studied an important chemical histamine which is produced in response to stress signals which make gaping holes in blood vessels producing signs of inflammation at that site. Histamine produces an itching response. This reaction is not produced elsewhere in the body because of the sophisticated chemical, signaling system's specificity. But when antihistamine drugs are given to reduce symptoms, they will go all over the body. In the brain histamine when released in response to stress signals will increase blood flow to nervous tissues ensuring a proper neurological processing required for survival when anti-histamine drugs are given, they suppress the cells producing histamine in the brain causing drowsiness.

According to Journal of American Medical Association Iatrogenic illness (caused by adverse reactions to prescribed drugs) is third leading cause of death in US. These are dismaying statistics for a healing profession that has arrogantly dismissed 3000 years of effective eastern medicine as unscientific even though it is based on deeper understanding of the universe.

In 2000 an article by V Pophristic[110] and L Goodman in the journal 'Nature' revealed that the laws of quantum physics and not Newtonian physics govern the molecules life generating movements.

Dr. Lipton[111] very aptly discuses an incident of which he was a witness while at Grad school. He held a job at an auto Garage. An irate woman drove in her car and complain regarding her service engine light flashing despite having it repaired several times. Everyone was quiet not wanting to address a problem on Friday evening. One mechanic agreed to solve the problem. He drove the car behind the bay, got behind the dashboard and removed the bulb from the signal light and threw it away so the light stopped flashing. The lady happily drove away not realizing that the cause was not addressed. Similarly pharmaceutical drugs address symptoms but not cause of disorders.

---

110 Biology of Belief by Dr. Bruce Lipton, Page 80
111 Biology of Belief by Dr. Bruce Lipton, Page 82

So, if we look at the tenth Dogma in Dr. Sheldrake's list, it says that 'Mechanistic medicine is the only one that works. This is not true. More and more people are opting for alternative medicine. A lot of research has been done in Ayurveda and Homeopathy. Both the knowledge systems have a lot to offer.

Professor Rama Jayasundara[112] (AIIMS) is a PhD from university of Cambridge (UK). She is trained in Physics and NMR (Nuclear Magnetic Resonance). She also has a degree in Ayurveda. I happened to listen to her very interesting talk on Ayurveda: Antiquated or state of Art.

She says that clinical medicine be it Allopathy, Ayurveda, Homeopathy they all begin with Diagnosis and end with treatment. Modern medicine supports Newtonian world view which believes that reality is made up of matter. It is a reductionist system where larger objects can be reduced to smaller ones.

Atoms --> molecules (DNA) --> organelle (nucleus) --> cell --> cardiac muscle tissue --> organ (Heart) --> Circulation system --> organism (several) systems.

So, the heart is considered a pump structure.

The biochemical tests done are also structure based and so are microbiological tests.

---

112 https://www.youtube.com/watch?v=-0-Df7CPB7E

The treatment strategies are based on rectifying structures or replacing structures. They are also based on supplementing deficiencies and chemical manipulation of structures. Modern medicine is Science of diseases, while Ayurveda is science of life.

Health is a complete balance of functioning of tissues their metabolic end products, senses, mind, consciousness and social, ecological wellbeing. Absence of disease is not health. According to Prof Jayasundara Ayurveda is an applied science and has inputs from all six Darshanas.

Another Enlightening talk on Ayurveda was by Dr. Ram Manohar[113] who is an Ayurveda expert and authority. He is the Research Director of Amruta school of Ayurveda [Amruta Vishwa Vidyapeetham] Kerala.

He says that Ayurveda is generally referred to as indigenous medicine or herbal medicine traditional medicine or else attached to vegetarianism. Ayurveda is a compound word separated as 'Ayus' and 'Veda' usually translated as Knowledge of life or Science of life.

Dr. Ram Manohar prefers not to use the word "Science" as it is a restricted word. Ayurveda is not closer to Medicine but is closer to Biology. 'Ayus' comes from Sanskrit words इन गदौ which means to go, disappear. Life is transient and will perish. गदौ means movement that is movement towards

---

113 https://www.youtube.com/watch?v=nA6ER8SYuos | https://www.youtube.com/watch?v=PxazSXOGER0

death. This is the paradox of life. Life is constantly adapting to survive. Entire focus of life processes is self-preservation. The three levels of survival are at Cellular level, Organism level and Spiritual level.

According to Ayurveda we can only prolong death. At Cellular level we are dying moment by moment. Prolongation is by self-reconstruction. Eating food is considered a Yagna for regeneration. Ayurveda gives a deep insight into life processes; its focus is to live life to its fullness and not only treating and healing a few diseases.

The work 'Veda' comes from root word 'Vid' meaning 'to know.'

'Vid' has four dimensions, the first being "सत्ता" one which exists and so one can observe it.

The second-dimension deals with conceptualization followed by analysis and finally experience.

Dr. Manohar says, Ayurveda is not about herbs. Anything under the sun is medicine. He related a very interesting story about Jivaka who was a student of Rishi Atreya. One fine day Atreya decided to test his students. He told them to go and search for plants that did not have any medicinal value. All students returned with plants except Jivaka. He told his Guru that he was unable to find a single plant without medicinal value. Atreya was very pleased with Jivaka and blessed him by saying, 'Now you are a doctor.' You have passed the test.

Anyone desiring a healthy life should study Ayurveda. In our tradition everyone had to learn Ayurveda to improve quality of life. Ayurveda is like a mirror you see yourself when you look into a mirror.

Ayurveda tells you what your uniqueness is in this world. Your whole existence is a finger print, a signature of what expresses through your life.

Further elaborating on Ayurveda Dr. Ram Manohar says that Indian tradition focuses on Consciousness. According to Ayurveda Body and Mind form a continuum. They are not separate. In west it is the body versus mind while in Ayurveda it is elf-versus non self. Every physical aspect is rooted in the mind so all diseases originate in mind. Ayurveda aims at healing the mind and the body gets healed automatically.

An ayurveda physician is one who can enter the mind of the patient and facilitate process of healing. In modern medicine there is a concept called 'Placebo Healing' which proves that mind has got tremendous healing potential. Modern medicine has not paid much attention to placebo effect while Ayurveda encourages placebo healing. Body is the grosser aspect of body mind continuum while mind is the subtler aspect. Through the body we are trying to control the mind and we fail. Ayurveda teaches us to take control of our mind. Mind being illusive we cannot see it but can infer it. Mind is the interface between Body and Self. Whatever we take from the body has the shadow of mind. (e.g., cells) On the other side of mind is Consciousness. When mind is hooked to Consciousness, we have a totally new experience. Through the body we can only see the shadow of mind. If we want to capture mind, we have to hook it with Consciousness. Ayurveda has derived its study from all shastras i.e., Vedas, Upanishads, Darshanas etc. We even find Buddhist thoughts. Ayurveda has multidimensional understanding of mind. It takes you on a journey of mental transformation. It takes you to the point where distinction between Self and non-Self ends, there is only Self. It is the end of all fears and anxieties and so is called 'Abha.'

According to Ayurveda "स्वस्थ" is a very insightful and esoteric word and cannot be equated with health. It means being with one's own awareness. So, when you are rooted in self you lose connection with body and to everything related to body.

In today's world we have PNI axis (Psychoneuroimmunological axis).

The Body has three doshas, Vata, Pitta, Kapha.

P   Psych – Mind
N   Neurological -> VATA
E   Endocrinological -> PITTA
I   Immunological -> KAPHA
Axis

Any disturbance in mind translates across PNEI Axis and produces disease. If mind is connected to Self-there is no disturbance in PNEI axis and this is "स्वस्थ" state. More the mind is attached to Self- more focused and centered it becomes and more powers are manifest through it. Turbulence in mind prevents one from exploring the higher dimensions. Interactions of sense organs with sense objects cause turbulence in mind.

The best time to wake up is Brahma Muhrata and this is for calibration of mind and expansion of consciousness. According to our scriptures a day is divided into six Yamas each of four hours. Brahma Muhrata is also called Saraswati Yama (from 2 am to 6 am). Just before the Saraswati Yama is the Kali Yama (10 pm to 2 am). This is the time we should be sleeping as it is time for self-repair of the body. This is the time melatonin increases and peaks. This is the time when one should switch off the lights as it interferes with working of melatonin and disturbs sleep cycles.

Food or Diet is also very important in Ayurveda because food supports mind and ultimately is responsible for production of 'OJAS' which nourishes the mind. Whatever we take inside does not nourish us. If we are physically dehydrated, we drink water.

What about mental dehydration? We must be very careful about our diet because whatever we eat must be conducive to expansion of mind. Mind is 'achetna' (not conscious) while heart is 'Chetna' (Conscious). Ayurveda considers head as seat of mind and heart as seat of consciousness. Mind is like a computer, but awareness is something totally different. Oxytocin also known as love hormone is released through heart. It is released by Pituitary gland. The love of a mother for her child is the best example one can give. This love is from the heart.

Dr. Manohar pointed out a very important aspect regarding love or connection through the heart. A person who has lost his mind finds it impossible to communicate with others. The only way he can connect is through the heart. If the mind connects to the body through the brain, one becomes more egoistic and body centric. Connection through the heart makes one less body centric. To remain healthy, one must connect to the Self.

The first step in this process of liberation starts with food we eat. The purity and quality of food is very important to complete the transformation that happens once food is injested. Food must be transformed into 'Ojas'. According to Bhagwat Geeta food stored more than 3 hour is 'tamasic. why? The life force of the food is destroyed. The movement of life force is always upwards. Degraded food moves down into Tamasic category. The digestive essence of food is called 'Rasa.' Rasa circulates in the body. The meaning of 'Rasa' in Sanskrit is essence and one that flows as it circulates in the body. Third meaning of 'Rasa' is one that burns. Vegetarian food has its source in plants and plants are called 'Aushaadha', 'dhi' meaning receptacle and 'ausha' meaning burning transformation. Plants are primary metabolizers of food. Without them no food would be available on the planet. Aushaadha is often mistaken as medicinal plants but all plants are called Aushaadha as they make their own food using chlorophyll and sunlight so whatever we eat is Aushaadha. The fifth meaning of rasa is bliss (to enjoy). Food leads you to this bliss. To experience bliss there must be complete transformation of food into Ojas. Ayurvedic medicines are all food supplements and so are called Aushaadha. When there is a failed transformation of food, medicine is given to restore the process. Function of Ayurvedic medicine is to awaken the mind. Aushaadha is one that awakens your Chetna.

Ayurveda's approach to healing is holistic. It is not structure based as in Allopathy. It delves deep down at energy levels and addresses cause of the disease or disorder. Ayurveda also refutes the eighth dogma listed by Dr. Sheldrake that mind is inside brain. Brain is more like a TV receiver and tunes into what is externally present just as I mentioned earlier.

Pondering on above 10 dogmas has opened a new horizon regarding life and its working. Dr. Sheldrake[114] says Morphic Resonance is a process whereby self-organizing systems inherit a memory from previous similar systems. Memory need not be stored in material traces in brains which are more like TV receivers than video recorders tuning into influences of the past. Biological inheritance need not all be coded in Genes or in epigenetic modification of genes. Much depends on Morphic Resonance from previous members of Species. Thus, everyone inherits a collective memory from past member of Species and contributes to collective memory affecting other members of the Species in future. Our intentions and thoughts do affect our environment both internal and external.

Since last so many years we are observing more and more scientists moving away from the age-old materialistic models and accepting the Quantum way. There has been a paradigm shift in the way we look at our universe. Physicists and Biologists are coming up with totally new ideas, concepts regarding

---

114 https://www.sheldrake.org/research/morphic-resonance

the universe, life and its workings backed up by experimental evidence. The more we read about these articles the more convinced we are regarding our ancient Indian wisdom, our scriptures and other manuscripts which are still unopened. When these manuscripts get deciphered and translated it will open venues unimagined.

We do not realize how much we are still trapped in the clutches of materialism. We are totally blind towards other concepts because we cannot perceive them with our sense organs. Dr. Lothar Schafer[115] in one of his talks mentioned that English language can brainwash us to believe in materialism. He gave an example of the word 'unimportant' meaning, it does not Matter. The other word he mentioned was Empty meaning Nothing (No, thing). He elaborated further by using a sentence in English "Lets discuss our differences objectively."

Dr. Schafer says, it is not possible because objectivity can be only to the extent one's language allows".

Coming back to the word 'empty' meaning 'nothing' is not right because it is filled with invisible forms. We are so much geared up to 'things', solid forms that it is difficult to believe in things without form.

---

[115] https://www.youtube.com/watch?v=jzafB6NKHis

English has one word for 'reality' while German has two words 'Realitat' and 'Wirklichkeit' which means one which will act on you even though you cannot see it. It is just up to the readers to wonder over the vastness depth and beauty of Sanskrit language when compared to English or any other language. Sanskrit words are based on levels of experience and so will allow a lot of freedom in usage and will succeed in conveying the idea or concept or thing in just the right way leaving no space for doubt. Dr. Schafer mentions in his talk about an allegory invented by Indian Sages where they put a thousand pots filled with water under sunlight and each pot had reflection of Sun but, there is only one Sun. Similarly, there is only one God or Cosmic Consciousness also known as Paramatma. Paramatma is all pervading in the universe and He sustains life. As we saw earlier in the Ishavasya Upanishad.

इशावास्यं इदं सर्व यत्किञ्चत् जगत्याम् जगत्

He is the sustainer and controller of our Universe.

This human life has a purpose and goal. We must rise above mundane desires and baser passions. We are all seekers of truth and it will not be revealed to us unless we are pure in thought and action.

Dr. APJ Abdul Kalam[116] writes in his last book Transcendence, "Becoming Good through repeated virtuous acts is the very reason and order of our human nature, for it is only in goodness that we penetrate mystique of our existence and behold a full human life. A pure man with his well-formed conscience understands that truth obligates him to pursue it at all costs. We are truth seekers as Pramukh Swamiji says, because this is precisely the way that God has lovingly created us.

---

116 Transcendence by Dr. Abdul Kalam, Page 188

Epilogue

I sincerely thank all who have journeyed with me till here in this book. We have indeed been endowed with a beautiful life. Being alive and being able to witness the marvelous world around us is a precious gift from God. We are naturally born to remain joyful and happy. The innermost essence of our existence is Sat-Chit-Ananda. Being in a state of Bliss is our Birth right. As Shri Krishna tells Arjuna in the Bhagavat Geeta.

कर्मण्येवाधिकारस्ते मा फलेषु कदाचिन ।
मा कर्मफलहेतुर्भूमा ते सङ्गोस्त्वकर्मणि ॥ 2/47

You are free to choose what to do (Karma) but it is not within your capacity to choose the fruits of your action. We live in this illusion of 'doer- ship' and so remain in the conflict stage. Happiness eludes us and sorrow arrives uninvited. We are in a state of pain and suffering only witnessing joy in fleeting moments. All of us yearn for Eternal peace and happiness yet it eludes us. Why is it so? We are looking for it in the wrong place. Looking for it in this material world will not give any hope. It sure does not exist there. This is what our shastras have revealed to us since thousands of years. Our Enlightened Gurus also utter the same truth.

For this peace and joy to materialize there is a need to cleanse our internal environment, our mind, our thoughts. We are busy tending the external aspect whether it be the body or our possessions. Our Goal is to achieve peace and joy but the way taken towards it leads us to pain and conflicts.

Our Culture, Traditions, Customs, Festivals, Shastras; which have been practiced and imbibed for thousands of years are a treasure house showing the road towards Eternal Peace, Bliss, and Joy. All we must do is to reconnect to this ancient wisdom which surely is an Antidote to today's issues, sorrows, and conflicts. This is the surest and shortest way to neutralize the poison.

Dr. Abdul Kalam[117] has beautifully said,

> "Where there is righteousness in heart,
> there is beauty in character, when
> there is beauty in character, there is

---

[117] Transcendence by Dr. Abdul Kalam, Page 81

harmony in the home, when there is harmony in the home, there is order in the nation and when there is order in the nation there is peace in the world.

All of this can be achieved by understanding and imbibing the lofty ideals, values, and rich heritage of our Culture whose proud inheritors we all are. A sincere affinity must be cultivated to delve deeper for more clear understanding of different aspects of our Culture. This way we Indians can contribute in a positive way towards amelioration of the world at large. We can remain rooted in our Culture and still be Global citizens.

I end by quoting these beautiful lines by Rabindranath Tagore.[118]

> "The most important lesson that man can learn from life is not that there is pain in this world but it is possible for him to transmute it into joy."

---

[118] https://www.goodreads.com/work/quotes/1922642-sadhana-the-realization-of-life?page=2

CPSIA information can be obtained
at www.ICGtesting.com
Printed in the USA
LVHW070510210223
740023LV00022B/1742